# THE NOAH'S ARK

# NONSENSE

In contrast to the institute's scholarly publications produced mainly for professors and advanced students, its Truth in Religion series is for laymen and the general public. The purpose of the series is to provide, on the popular level, the results of the best scholarship on the subjects. Emphasis will be placed on presenting the truth--in the institute's judgment--on topics on which much misinformation and misunderstanding are prevalent.

Number 1 in the series examines the nature and promotion of the claim that Noah's ark is on Mount Ararat.

Number 2, planned for publication in 1979, will be entitled The Historical Approach to the Bible. Written by the same author, it will be a survey of the development of that approach and an introduction to the use of its principles in understanding the Bible.

# THE NOAH'S ARK NONSENSE

### HOWARD M. TEEPLE

RELIGION AND ETHICS INSTITUTE, INC.

1978

L. C.: 78-53529
ISBN: 0-914384-01-5

Published by
Religion and Ethics Institute, Inc.
P.O. Box 664
Evanston, Illinois, U.S.A. 60204

Printed in the United States of America by
Edwards Brothers, Inc.
Ann Arbor, Michigan 48104

TO

the historians and
archaeologists who
have uncovered the
real nature of the
story of the Flood

# THE INSTITUTE

The Religion and Ethics Institute was incorporated
under the laws of the state of Illinois as a nonprofit cor-
poration 29 November 1972. The purpose of the institute, as stated in its charter, is "to promote the discovery and distribution of sound historical and scientific
knowledge in the fields of religion and ethics." The institute proposes to do this through both discovery on
the research level and distribution on the popular level.

# PREFACE

With astonishment I learned last December from its advance promotion that NBC was going to present a film that claimed that Noah's ark is on Mount Ararat. When I watched the program, the astonishment was transformed into shock. As a former believer in religious fundamentalism, I quickly recognized the old "party line." The documentary format of the film, together with some of its statements, appeared to give factual support for the fundamentalist doctrine, "the Bible is true," meaning, the whole Bible is literally the word of God. I soon decided that, besides protesting to NBC, I would write a book to set the record straight.

The book could not have been written without the assistance of others, whose help is gratefully acknowlledged. Dr. Wolfgang Roth, professor of Old Testament at Garrett-Evangelical Theological Seminary, encouraged me to undertake this project and gave assistance. My wife Gladys aided in many ways. In addition to giving her moral support, she assisted in collecting material, gave rigorous criticism of the manuscript, and typed most of the final form for printing by photo-offset. Dr. Arnold Nelson of Winston-Salem, a member of the Board of Directors of the Religion and Ethics Institute, read and criticized chapters 1 to 11. The following libraries were used in addition to my own: Garrett-Evangelical Theological Seminary, Newberry, Northwestern University, Seabury-Western Theological Seminary, and the University of Chicago. NBC granted permission to publish our correspondence. Finally, a special note of appreciation to Emery Communications, whose cover drawing aptly symbolizes the slippage and fall of the notion that Noah's ark is on Mount Ararat.

Evanston
August 6, 1978

H. M. T.

# CONTENTS

THE PROBLEM

THE FLOOD

THE ARK

THE MEDIA

# CHAPTER 1

## INCREDIBLE REGRESSION

Sometimes you don't know whether to laugh or cry! Sometimes things happen that are so ridiculous that you want to laugh. Yet their effects are so tragic that you want to cry.

Such is the case with the Noah's ark craze. The unsubstantiated claims made in connection with the theory that there is an ark on Mount Ararat, the excuses made to explain how Noah could have gotten all those animals on an ark and fed them for a year, and the rationalizations made by the proponents of this nonsense, is enough to make a genuine historian explode with laughter. But the results are no laughing matter. The consequent misunderstanding of the nature of the Bible, the intolerant attitude toward scientists and historians, and the retardation of intellectual growth in religion are utterly tragic in their effects upon society.

Beginning with the church fathers, traditional Christianity through the centuries defended the faith in the historical accuracy of the biblical stories, including the story of a universal Flood and Noah's ark. Judaism, too, accepted the stories in the Hebrew Scriptures, which Christians labeled the "Old Testament." But religious leaders in the past lacked knowledge of the nature of the Bible: the process of its literary formation, the situation of its writers, and the influence of the environment. In the last two centuries the research by historians, biblical scholars, archaeologists (many of whom were Christians or Jews) revolutionized mankind's understanding of the biblical narratives. One of the results of their research is the recognition of the fictional character of some accounts. Another result is the discovery that the story was not original with the Hebrews, but was borrowed by them from their neighbors and revised.

Two different types of reaction to the historical research occurred in both Judaism and Christianity. Many Jews and Christians adjusted to the new knowledge and no longer regarded belief in the Flood as essential. Today the standard commentaries on Genesis and the main dictionaries of the Bible accept the results of the research, and so do the professors generally in mainline seminaries. John H. Marks has summed up the situation: "The belief in a deluge covering the whole earth and destroying all men and animals except those preserved in an ark has been largely given up."[1]

The other type of reaction was negative and defensive. Some individuals and religious groups, especially some Christians who became known as "fundamentalists," denounced the new knowledge, feeling that it was their duty to "defend the Bible." Various zealots wrote articles and books to try to show the plausibility of a universal Flood and a huge ancient ark that would hold a pair of all kinds of animals, birds, and creeping things, along with the provisions necessary to feed them. In 1931 B. C. Nelson attempted to use geology to defend belief in the Flood.[2] The same author had previously written a book to defend belief in the biblical Creation story.[3]

A special form of the apologetic effort to uphold the Flood story and the Bible in general was the eagerness to climb Mount Ararat and find the ark there. This motive became a virtual mania with some persons in the nineteenth and twentieth centuries. The situation led the French archaeologist, André Parrot, who was the Director of the Louvre Museum, to write a brief exposé of the ark nonsense.[4] For some people, Noah's ark became the modern Crusaders' Holy Grail! Some recent books report the efforts to find the ark on Mount Ararat, and they attempt to uphold the faith that re-

mains of the ark are up there.  A pioneer work of this
type was written by J. W. Montgomery in 1972. [5]  Several similar books quickly followed (see "Selected Bibliography" below).  The book written by D. Balsiger and
C. E. Sellier, Jr., was published in 1976 by a subsidiary
of Sun Classic Pictures, which made a film of the same
name, "In Search of Noah's Ark." [6]  The film has the
framework of an investigative documentary, but actually
it presents only a fundamentalist point of view, namely,
literal interpretation of the Bible, faith in the historicity of the Flood, and belief that the ark is on Mount Ararat.  The evidence to the contrary is omitted, yet that
evidence is surely important, for it is the evidence that
has convinced biblical scholars and historians.  The
leading authorities on the subject are not even mentioned.
The film gives the impression that "historians, archaeologists, scholars" generally agree with its conclusions,
whereas the real situation is just the opposite.

On December 24, 1977, the National Broadcasting
Company televised that film nationally in prime time.
The film had already been televised nationally in the
summer of the same year.  NBC gave the Christmas
Eve presentation spot advertising for about a week in
advance.  There was no hint either in the promotion or
in the actual program that it was a sectarian approach
to the subject.  After monitoring the Christmas Eve
telecast, the Religion and Ethics Institute first protested
to NBC, then later filed a formal complaint with the
Federal Communications Commission.

Considering the tremendous growth in the understanding of the Flood story and the significant transfor-
mation of the interpretation of the Bible that have occurred in the last hundred years, it is amazing to find the
clock of knowledge turned backward on such a large
scale!  Historians thought the matter was settled.  Some
orthodox reaction against the historical understanding of
the Bible has always been with us in modern times, but

at least the public knew whence it came.  When the presentation of obsolete views pretends to be the result of
new, objective investigation, and when the whole subject
is distorted to make it sensational, we should become
alarmed.  That approach is the utter antithesis of scholarship.  The most shocking of all, however, is the tele-
casting nationally of sectarian views in the disguise of a
documentary.  This seductive device could be used to
foster all kinds of propaganda: political, social,  and
economic, as well as religious.

The history of the Flood story and of the efforts to
find the ark are interesting in themselves.  But the recent intense interest in the subject involves much more
than appears on the surface.  The current Noah's ark
nonsense epitomizes two serious problems that are
underneath, one in religion and one in the media.

The time has come to take a close look at this whole
matter.  Let us first uncover the basic religious problem, then examine the history of the Flood story and the
efforts to find the ark, and finally look at the threat from
the media.

# CHAPTER 2

## THE FUNDAMENTAL PROBLEM

Before we examine the Noah's ark nonsense, we should locate the real problem and bring it out into the open. The basic problem involved is not the interpretation of archaeological, geological, or literary evidence, but rather, the interpretation of the Bible. It is the FUNDAMENTALIST approach to the Bible that is the FUNDAMENTAL problem. As we use the term "fundamentalist," we are not referring to particular sects, but to an ultraconservative point of view in respect to the Bible. What is the fundamentalist approach?

## ATTITUDE TOWARD THE BIBLE

The fundamentalist approach begins with the presupposition that God inspired the whole Bible verbatim, so that every word of it is literally "God's word." Therefore the fundamentalists are obsessed with the faith that "the Bible is true." This belief seems so important to fundamentalists that they regard it as a fundamental, or necessary, doctrine that every person should accept. Although a story that the Bible plainly presents as a story (for example, the Parable of the Prodigal Son) is recognized as fiction, any story in a historical framework is stoutly defended by them as literal history. This includes the story of the Flood.

The attitude that the whole Bible must be true leads to the opinion that there can be no factual errors and no contradictions in the Bible. They who hold this opinion either ignore or oppose the suggestion that the biblical Flood story contains contradictions.

Fundamentalists also assume that it is necessary to accept the traditional authorship of the biblical books. Accordingly they assert that Moses wrote Genesis because tradition says he did, and the apostle John wrote the Gospel of John because tradition claims that he did. Consequently the fundamentalists reject the idea that some biblical books are composite and incorporate written sources or have been revised later by the scribes who copied and transmitted them to future generations. Needless to say, they do not like the idea that two Flood stories are interwoven in Genesis.

The attitude that the truth of the Bible and of the traditions about it are vital for religious faith makes fundamentalists very zealous to protect their view of the Bible. So they attack scientists for not believing the Creation story, historians for placing the Bible in its historical setting, and biblical scholars for upsetting traditional beliefs.

They who intensely desire to defend the authority of the Bible tend to react against modern understanding of that book by becoming "eager believers," if I may coin a term. They are so zealous to defend their view that they eagerly believe anything that seems to support their beliefs. The story of the Flood and Noah's ark is a case in point. The arguments used to support the belief that the Flood actually occurred are unsound and often ridiculous. The same is true of the claims made for evidence of the ark on Mount Ararat. The nature of the arguments is described below in chapters 7 and 10.

Sometimes the ark enthusiasts plainly reveal their religious motivation. Sometimes they frankly state their deep concern to support the trustworthiness of the whole Bible. Sometimes they incorporate a section or a chapter which argues that the Bible is historically accurate. [7]

The biased attitude which determines in advance that the Bible must all be true, regardless of evidence, is contrary to the objective attitude that is a basic principle of sound scholarship. The evidence should determine the nature of the conclusions, rather than the conclusions determining nature of the evidence.

Prejudiced attitudes have often been defended by re-marking that everyone has prejudices and therefore it is impossible to have an objective attitude. That remark overlooks the distinction between opinion and prejudice. Everyone has opinions, but he who has an objective at-titude will change his opinion in the light of new evidence. The mind controlled by a prejudiced attitude, however, will not be moved by evidence.

## METHOD OF INTERPRETATION

The fundamentalists' attitude toward the Bible deter-mines their method of interpreting it. One feature of their method is the screening out of evidence they dislike. When contradictions are encountered in the Bible, one statement may be accepted and the conflicting statement ignored. An example is the question of how many animals of a kind were taken aboard the ark in the Flood story. God's instruction to Noah to take two of each kind (Gen. 6:19) is readily accepted, while the contradictory instruc-tion to take seven pairs of birds and seven pairs of clean animals (Gen. 7:2-3) is usually ignored. If someone does call attention to such details, he is liable to be denounced for "picking the Bible to pieces." Actually, the failure to consider all the evidence is a violation of another basic principle of scholarship. The only way really to under-stand the Bible is to consider all the evidence, both in-side and outside it.

Another feature of the fundamentalists' method is the reinterpretation, or misinterpretation, of biblical pas-sages to make the Bible agree with their beliefs. When geology proved that the earth is much older than biblical chronology would make it, some persons tried to ex-plain away the discrepancy by saying that a "day" in the Creation story might be a long period of time. Not only is there no evidence for this interpretation, but the days in the story are plainly days in the ordinary sense be-

cause God blessed the seventh day as a day of rest  (Gen.
2:3), clearly a reference to the seventh day of the week.

A related feature of the fundamentalists' method is
the effort to twist evidence outside the Bible to support
their beliefs about the Bible.   Various uses of this device will appear when we examine, in chapter 7, the fundamentalist treatment of the Flood story.

A popular form of twisting outside evidence is the
misuse of archaeology to force it to support the historical accuracy of the Bible.  This practice is engaged in
not only by fundamentalists, but also by various writers
and occasionally even by archaeologists themselves for
the sake of producing something sensational.   A statement once made by Millar Burrows of Yale University is
well worth quoting:

> The distinction between fact and interpreta-
> tion is of the greatest importance for the bear-
> ing of archeological evidence on the meaning
> and value of the Bible.  Popular writers and
> speakers loosely use such expressions as that
> "archeology proves" this and that, which is
> like saying that science or history proves a
> proposition.  What is cited as proved by arch-
> eology is frequently some individual's inter-
> pretation, rather than anything clearly and
> certainly shown by the evidence itself.   The
> fact that the excavator himself may be respon-
> sible for the interpretation does not guarantee
> its truth.  Excavators, being human, some-
> times adopt too readily interpretations which
> make their discoveries seem especially im-
> portant. [8]

Sir Charles Marston, Werner Keller, and others
wrote books to defend the traditional view of the Bible,
using archaeology as evidence.  Even the famous Jewish archaeologist, Nelson Glueck, was too eager to find

archaeological support for the Old Testament.   On the other hand, books by Frederic Kenyon, Millar Burrows, André Parrot, and others represent honest, accurate use of archaeology in the interpretation of the Bible. The truth is that some archaeological evidence supports the Bible, but other archaeological discoveries disagree with it.


## EFFECTS OF FUNDAMENTALISM

When belief in the literal truth of the whole Bible becomes essential in religion, that religion is placed on a very shaky foundation.  It is easily demonstrated that the Bible is a human product of its time, containing some history, some fiction, some borrowing from neighboring religions, some truth, some errors, and some contradictions.  The content of the Bible naturally includes some ideas prevalent in the ancient world that are contrary to modern knowledge, ranging from the notion that the world was flat ("four corners of the earth, " Isa. 11:12 and Rev. 7:1), to belief in angels, to the mythological idea that when the Hebrews raised a great shout, the Lord caused the walls of Jericho to fall (Josh. 6:20).  Many undesirable effects result from making the truth of religion dependent upon the truth of such notions:

1.  A low standard for religion is set.  Religion is forced to continue to contain some of the superstitions and ignorance of the ancient past.  A distorted sense of values in religion results when unimportant or erroneous beliefs are regarded as of equal value with religious principles and ethics.

2.  Much modern knowledge and many ideals are shut out of religion because they are not in the Bible. Intelligent development of religion is blocked.

3.  Misunderstanding of the Bible itself is a consequence.  The nature of the Bible, the religious development within it, and the relation of the Bible to the total

history of religion are hidden from view by the fundamen-
alist approach. For example, within the Old Testament
there is a shift from the narrow racism in Ezra and Ne-
hemiah to the broad universalism in Second Isaiah (Isa.
40-55) and Jonah. Treating the whole Bible as literally
the word of God prevents its readers from understanding
the variety and development within it.

4. Often the noblest passages of the Bible are not
given a fair chance to speak to us today because they are
equated with inferior passages. Belief in the unity of the
Bible obscures the fact that sometimes a biblical writer
was trying to elevate religion to a higher plane than the
level in some other biblical books. Second Isaiah's effort to promote universalism is an example.

5. The unreasonable claims and conjectures made
to protect the belief in the literal truth of the whole Bible
tend to bring religion into disrepute in the sight of the
general public. Religion is ill-served by this. The wild
claims include those made to support belief in the Flood
and the ark.

Now we know the reason for the zealous promotion
of the faith in "the truth" of the Flood story and the belief that the ark is on Mount Ararat. The reason is not
the discovery of archaeological or historical evidence.
Instead, the reason is the ultraconservative desire to
"defend the Bible." It is not an accident that the American fundamentalists are the people who have organized
almost all the ark-hunting expeditions since World War
II. [8a]

# CHAPTER 3

## WHERE THE STORY BEGAN

Where did the Flood story originate? Why was it written? How did it get in the Bible? To answer these questions, we must turn to archaeology.

## THE SUMERIAN FLOOD TABLET

At the close of the nineteenth century the University of Pennsylvania excavated the site of the ancient Sumerian city of Nippur, in modern Iraq. The city, on the west bank of the Euphrates River, was the center of the national cult of the Earth-god, Enlil, from whom all the rulers of the cities of the lands of Sumer and Akkad derived their authority. The river has since changed its course, but in ancient times the Tigris and the Euphrates Rivers were closer to each other, and the fertile land between them was irrigated by running water across from the Euphrates to the Tigris. Nippur's position as a religious center and its location amidst great agricultural production made it a prosperous city. Sumerian civilization began in the fifth millenium B.C. or earlier, and was flourishing by 3500 B.C.

Among the thousands of clay tablets inscribed in cuneiform writing that were found when Nippur was excavated were those of the large library of the temple. The library contained documents of Sumerian literature and the records of the temple priests. In 1914 Arno Poebel, the leading Sumerologist of the day, published the text of the Flood story in poetic form that was on a fragment of one of the tablets. The tablet, inscribed in six columns, consists of only the bottom third of the tablet, and thus provides only a third of

each column.  The remainder of this Sumerian story has
not yet been found.  The date of the tablet is around 1600
B. C. [9]  It is now located in the University Museum of
the University of Pennsylvania.

The surviving portion of the first column on the Sumerian fragment starts with the last part of a speech which,
apparently, is delivered by one deity to an assembly of
deities.  The speaker announced that after he stops the
destruction of "my human race, " he wants the people to
return to their cities and rebuild them "on holy places. "
The speaker claims that he has perfected the divine laws.
He wants that there be peace and that the land be irrigated.  The column closes with a brief statement of the creation of "the blackheaded people, " vegetation, and four-
legged animals of the plain.  The creation was accom-
plished by four gods:  An, Enlil, Enki, and Ninhursag.

Then follows the lacuna, or gap in the text, caused
by the loss of the upper section of the tablet, after which
the story continues in the lower portion of the second column.  The authority of kings is supported by the statement that kingship has been lowered from heaven.  The
god who perfected the divine laws has founded five Sumerian cities; he gave them names and assigned a ruler
over each.  He established the cleaning of the small canals and the irrigation ditches.

The text in the next lacuna evidently reported the
decision of the gods in their assembly to bring a Flood
upon the earth and wipe out mankind.  The surviving
portion of the third column tells us that some of the deities, including Inanna, wept for the people.  Then we are
introduced to Ziusudra, a humble, reverent king, who
seeks divine revelation.

The fourth column continues by relating that Ziusudra stood by a wall where he heard the voice of a deity
who informed him that by the decision of the gods in assembly, a Flood will sweep over the cities to destroy
the seed of mankind.  Also, by the word spoken by the
gods An, Enlil, and Ninhursag, the kingship will be

overthrown.

The text in the lacuna that follows must have reported that Ziusudra built a huge boat, probably according
to divine instructions.    The surviving part of the fifth
column describes him in the boat during the storm, after which the Sun-god, Utu, shone forth, presumably
drying up the water.    In appreciation, the king sacrificed to the Sun-god.    This important section of the
text reads as follows:

> All the destructive winds (and) gales were
>     present,
> The storm swept over the capitals.
> After the storm had swept the country for
>     seven days and seven nights
> And the destructive wind had rocked the
>     huge boat in the high water,
> The Sun came out, illuminating the earth
>     and sky,
> Ziusudra made an opening in the huge boat,
> And the Sun with its rays entered the huge
>     boat.
> The king Ziusudra
> Prostrated himself before the Sun-god,
> The king slaughtered a large number of
>     bulls and sheep. [10]

In the passage above "capitals" refers to the cities, the
cult centers.    The Sun is the Sun-god, whom the king
worships ("prostrated himself before") and to whom he
sacrifices bulls and sheep.

The surviving portion of the sixth column tells us
that Ziusudra prostrated himself before the gods An
and Enlil, who gave him "eternal life, like a god," because he had preserved the "seed of mankind."    They
settled him in an overseas country, in "Dilmun," in
the east.

In the complete Sumerian text the Flood probably

was only a chapter in a sort of history of mankind, a history which described the creation of man, the building of cities, and the establishment of kingship. [11]

"Ziusudra" apparently is not the name of a real king, but an ideal king, for the name is derived from his role in the story. The name means "he saw life," a reference to his obtaining everlasting life after the Flood.

## THE ORIGIN OF THE STORY

Where did the Flood story originate? Sumer appears to be the locale. At least the Sumerian Nippur tablet, the earliest-known document of the story, was found there and is written in the Sumerian language. The text mentions canals and irrigation ditches, which were particularly characteristic of that region. Further, the story must have originated in an area where the people had experienced floods, or at least had observed that heavy windstorms could cause floods. Sudden rains in the mountains could cause floods in the valley, and if there was heavy rain in the valley at the same time, the likelihood that rivers and canals would overflow their banks was increased. In contrast to Sumer and Babylonia, Palestine was not a region where wide floods occurred.

When did the Flood story originate? As we have seen, the date of the Sumerian Nippur tablet is around 1600 B. C. However, Gudea, king of the Sumerian city-state of Lagash in the twenty-second century B.C., mentioned "the Flood of Enlil." [12] The story probably existed by the middle of the third millenium B.C.

When the Babylonian Gilgamesh Epic (see next chapter) was discovered, historians thought at first that it was the original story, but later, when the Sumerian story was discovered, the Sumerian was recognized as the older. Not only is the date of the Sumerian tablet earlier, but its story has more primitive, unde-

veloped characteristics--a trait typical of the earlier versions of stories.

Further evidence that the Sumerian story is earlier
than the Babylonian is the fact that the Sumerian contains
no Babylonian features, but the Babylonian has retained
some Sumerian features.  In all the Babylonian accounts
of the Flood, the Sumerian god Enlil is still the chief god,
and the Babylonian god Marduk is not even mentioned.
Only Sumerian gods are in the Sumerian story.  Obviously the Babylonian stories are later than, but derived from,
the Sumerian.

What was the purpose of the story ?  Why was it composed in the first place ?  Judging from the surviving fragments of the text, the purpose was two-fold: to support
the authority of kings (by claiming that kingship was ap-
pointed by the gods in heaven) and to support the priests
and their cult.  The second motive is indicated by the
concern for building the cities "on holy places" and for
the promotion of the divine laws.  The two motives are
closely related, for the king was divine and the head of
the cult.  The government was a theocracy, and kings and
priests were interdependent on each other.  Ziusudra is
saved from the flood and rewarded with immortal life
among the gods because he is a pious king who fears and
actively supports them.  The poet who composed the story may have been attached to a royal court.

As the late Professor Cassuto observed, in ancient
Mesopotamia great importance was attached to the story
of the Flood. [13]  It was a favorite subject with Sumerian
poets, and their epics formed the basis for other writers
to list the kings in two categories: antediluvian and post-
diluvian (i.e., before the Flood and after the Flood).  The
popularity of the story was undoubtedly a factor in its
widespread diffusion later into other lands.

# CHAPTER 4

## THE STORY MOVED NORTH

In the ancient world, literature spread from one country to another, and some stories, poems, and proverbs were especially popular. Often writers modified and expanded the literature by changing names and substituting ideas to make it fit into their own environment. Adaptation of material from other cultures to make it useful in the later writers' own culture was a common practice. In spite of the modifications, literary dependence of the later writer upon the earlier is often apparent through the preservation of some features and even words.

When people in other countries learned of the story of the Flood, they liked it too. The story is dramatic. The notion of only a few people surviving a general disaster has its appeal, even today. Modern examples are the stories of a few survivors of a nuclear war or an attack from outer space. Another reason for the story's continuing popularity is that it was easily adapted to the promotion of various ideas.

The spread of the Sumerian story to other cultures began with its adoption by the Babylonians, among whom it circulated widely. The non-Semitic Sumerians were conquered by their northern Semitic neighbors, led by Sargon I of Akkad (or Accad or Agade) in the middle of the third millenium B. C. After the rise and fall of various dynasties, the Semite Hammurabi founded the Babylonian empire by extending his rule over the regions of both Akkad and Sumer late in the nineteenth century B. C. Akkadian (Old Babylonian) language and writing replaced the Sumerian, but the Babylonians adopted much of the Sumerian religion and literature.

The popularity of the Flood story among the Babylonians is demonstrated by the number of tablets con-

taining it that have been found.    There must have been
also many tablets which have not yet been discovered or
have been destroyed.    Additional evidence of the story's
popularity is the presence of variations in the accounts.
Enough Babylonian writers became interested in the story to modify it and expand it;   the story was not merely
copied routinely by scribes.


## THE BABYLONIANS

### Atrahasis

Atrahasis is an Old Babylonian revision of the Sumerian Flood story.   In it the survivor has the Babylonian
name Atrahasis instead of the Sumerian name Ziusudra.
The name Atrahasis, too, is derived from the hero's
role in the story.   The name means "the exceeding wise,"
and the man apparently was saved because of his wisdom.
From 1849 to 1854 the British excavated the site of
Nineveh.   They discovered there thousands of clay tablets, inscribed in cuneiform, belonging to the library of
Ashurbanipal, king of Assyria in the ninth century B. C.
At first the tablets  did not seem very valuable, for the
key to deciphering them was unknown.   The excavators
piled the tablets into baskets and shipped them to the
British Museum, where they arrived in broken condition.   In 1857 Sir Henry C. Rawlinson and others discovered how to translate the Babylonian and Assyrian languages.   While George Smith, a young assistant in the
museum, was repairing damaged tablets in 1872,  he
recognized on a tablet an Old Babylonian account of the
Flood and translated it.   Thus the modern world learned
of the existence of two Babylonian versions of the
Deluge story, Atrahasis and one incorporated in the
Gilgamesh Epic.   As Smith found it, Atrahasis was very
incomplete; more of it has become known gradually,
from 1872 to 1969, as additional fragments of clay
tablets containing portions of it have been found and

published.

The Babylonian versions demonstrate that after Babylon conquered Sumer, the Babylonians adopted the story.
They show, too, that the story continued to move northward, to the royal Assyrian library at Nineveh in northern Mesopotamia. W. G. Lambert dates the <u>Atrahasis</u>
tablets around 1600 B. C. [14] Large portions of the <u>Atra-
hasis</u> story are still missing, but in the fragments we
have, the story runs as follows.

Originally the gods were alone in the universe; Anu's
domain was heaven, Enlil's was earth, and Enki's was
Apsu ("the Deep"), the body of water under the earth that
was the source of the springs on earth. The great gods
put the lesser gods to work digging canals and producing
crops, but after forty years of such hard work, they re-
belled. So the great gods decided to create mankind to
do the work. A god was slaughtered and his flesh and
blood mixed with clay, so "that god and man may be thor-
oughly mixed in the clay." Fourteen birth goddesses took
some of it, and at the beginning of the tenth month they
gave birth to fourteen humans, seven males and seven
females.

The human race multiplied and made so much noise
that Enlil could not sleep. He decided to reduce their
numbers by sending a plague. The king Atrahasis appealed to Enki for help, who by indirect means stopped
the plague. Again mankind multiplied and made so much
noise that Enlil could not sleep, so he caused a drought
on earth. Atrahasis again prayed to Enki, who induced
the storm god Adad to send rain without Enlil's knowledge. Once more mankind multiplied and became noisy,
so Enlil tried a second drought. A gap in the text follows, but apparently the drought was ended again by Enki,
who had a whirlwind pick up fish from his domain, the
cosmic sea under the earth, and drop them on the earth
for mankind to eat. The great gods decided that never
again should a god save humanity. Enki only roared
with laughter. The gods tried to bind Enki with an oath

to comply with their decision, but he refused. Thereupon
Enlil decided to destroy the human race by means of the
Flood.

In a missing section the god Enki evidently gave Atrahasis a dream as a warning of the impending Flood. Then
the story continues in the surviving portion of the text.
Atrahasis asked "his lord" to teach him the meaning of
the dream.  Enki replied to "his slave," "Destroy your
[reed] house, build a boat [with the material], spurn
property and save life."  Enki told him to put a roof over
it so that the sun will not shine inside it. Atrahasis should
put pitch on the boat to make it strong and waterproof.
Enki announced to him that the Flood will come on the
seventh night. King Atrahasis assembled the elders and
told them that his god (Enki, the god of the subterranean waters) and their god (Enlil, the god of the earth)
are angry with each other and have expelled him from
the earth.  He told them that because he worships Enki, that god has told him of the matter.  Atrahasis said
that consequently he cannot stay in Enlil's domain, the
earth (and therefore he will build a boat so that he can
live in Enki's watery domain).  The carpenters and
reed-workers built the boat; children brought the pitch,
and poor men brought other material.  Atrahasis caught
clean animals and fat animals and put them on board,
along with birds, cattle, and wild creatures.  He invited
his people to a banquet, but sent his family on board the
ship.  He himself was restless, ill, and his heart was
broken (because of the impending fate of his people).

Then the weather changed and the storm god Adad
roared in the clouds.  Atrahasis closed the door of his
boat and sealed it with pitch; he cut the howser and set
the boat adrift.  The Flood came and destroyed the people.  There was no sun, and darkness prevailed.  The
gods were very disturbed at the destruction, and the
mother goddess, Mami, asked herself why, in the assembly of the gods, she had agreed to total destruction.  She denounced Enlil for uttering abominable evil

(i. e., ordering the destruction of life). She lamented that
her offspring (humanity) have been cut off from her. The
birth goddess Nintu wept, and the other gods wept with
her.  The storm and Deluge lasted for seven days and
seven nights.

The portion of the clay tablet containing the next
thirty-eight lines is missing.  The surviving text begins again by reporting that Atrahasis made an offering
to the gods, who smelled it and gathered around and ate
it.  Nintu complained against all the other gods for trying to destroy humanity.  She grieved, and vowed that
she would remember the disaster forever.  Then Enlil
saw the boat, and angrily asked how mankind had survived.  Anu remarked that only Enki could be the one
responsible for it.  Without hesitation Enki admitted
his role in the matter.

The remaining two and a half columns of the tablet
are in very fragmentary condition.  Perhaps in the missing portions Atrahasis became immortal after the Flood.
Someone, probably Enki, suggested that the gods could
impose a penalty on whomever disregards the command
of their assembly.  Enlil asked that Enki and the birth
goddess confer on the future of the peoples, with special concern for the subject of childbirth.  The story
ends with this statement: "I have sung of the Flood to
all the peoples.  Hear it."

In the introduction to their publication of the text,
Lambert and Millard conclude--rightly, I believe--
that Atrahasis is not an epic poem, but a song that was
sung publicly. [15]

The Semitic Flood Tablet from Nippur

A Semitic fragment found at Nippur, inscribed in
Old Babylonian, states that the name of the boat to be
built will be "Saver of Life."  The boat is to have a
strong roof or covering, and "beasts of the field and
birds of the heavens" are to be put aboard.  This frag-

ment apparently is a portion of Atrahasis or a story based
on it.

## The Gilgamesh Epic

Some Babylonian poets had produced a long story
about a hero, Gilgamesh, king of the city Uruk (called
Erech in Genesis 10:10), in southern Babylonia.    They
incorporated the Flood story in this Gilgamesh Epic, as
it is called.  Lambert and Millard observed that this
version of the story apparently was derived from Atrahasis, probably through the intermediary of a Middle
Babylonian edition. [16]  Some Babylonian changes have
been made in the names in the Flood in the Gilgamesh
Epic.  Here the builder of the ark is called Uta-napishtim, or Utnapishtim, a Babylonian translation of the
Sumerian name Ziusudra.   The god who warns him is
Ea, which is the Babylonian name for the Sumerian god
Enki. The framework of the Flood story in the epic is
that Gilgamesh becomes very worried about death after
his close friend dies;  he travels far to find Uta-napishtim and ask him how he became immortal.

Uta-napishtim told Gilgamesh that he will reveal to
him a secret of the gods; then he proceeded to relate the
story of the Flood.  According to this version of the story, Ea told Uta-napishtim, by means of a dream,  that
the great gods have decided to produce the Flood.   Ea
instructed him to tear down his house and build a ship
with it, to abandon his possessions, and to take aboard
"the seed of all living things."   Acting on Ea's advice,
Uta-napishtim deceived the people of his city by telling
them that a rain is coming which will bring them  an
abundance of harvest.  This deceit prevented the people
from becoming frightened and building arks of their own
to save themselves.  (The deceit, apparently, is a literary device to explain why other people did not build
boats too.)   Oil and bitumen were used to caulk  and
seal the boat.  The ship had an acre of floor space and

was a cube: ten dozen (Babylonian) cubits (about 200 feet) high, ten dozen cubits wide, and ten dozen cubits long. The ship had a total of seven decks, with each deck divided into nine sections. Thus there were 63 compartments (7 x 9). At one point in the story this ark is referred to as a "large house."

Uta-napishtim furnished the workmen with an abundance of meat and wine, and on the seventh day the ark was completed. The launching of the ship "was very difficult" (launching a huge cube probably would be!). Uta-napishtim put on board his family, relatives, livestock, the craftsmen, the boatman, and the "wild creatures of the field." He evidently took birds too, for before the boat landed, he sent some forth. He seems to have forgotten the divine command to abandon his possessions, however, for he loaded the ship with whatever he had of silver and gold! When the weather became frightening, he boarded the boat and tightly closed the entrance. Adad, the god of storm and rain, thundered; the "south-storm" blew, producing a cloudburst for six days and nights. Ninurta, the god of wells and irrigation, caused the dikes to burst.

Even the gods were frightened by the terrible Deluge; they ascended to the heaven of Anu, the Sumerian sky-god, where they "cowered like dogs, crouched against the outer wall." Ishtar (the Babylonian name for Inanna, the Sumerian goddess of love and childbirth) moaned and asked herself:

> How could I bespeak evil in the Assembly
> of the gods,
> Ordering battle for the destruction of my
> people,
> When it is I myself who give birth to my
> people!

The other deities wept too.

On the seventh day the south-storm subsided, the

sea became quiet, and the Flood ceased. "And all of mankind had returned to clay." Uta-napishtim opened a hatch,
then sat and wept (for mankind). The boat had landed on
Mount Nisir in the Zagros Mountains. On the seventh day
after the landing, Uta-napishtim sent forth a dove, but it
found no resting place and returned. He sent forth a swal-
low, and it came back. Then he sent forth a raven, which,
seeing that the waters had diminished, did not come back.
Uta-napishtim freed his living cargo and on the mountain
top offered a sacrifice to the gods. They smelled the
sweet savor and "crowded like flies" around him. Ishtar
vowed never to forget "these days," and declared that
the god Enlil should not come to the offering because he,
"unreasoning," had brought on the Deluge and consigned
her people to destruction.

Nevertheless, Enlil arrived at the sacrifice and
was angry that man had survived the Flood. Then Ea
asked "valiant Enlil" how could he, "the wisest of the
gods," be so unreasoning and cause the Deluge? Then
follows a beautiful scene. Enlil reversed his attitude,
took Uta-napishtim by the hand and led him with his wife
aboard the boat, touched their foreheads and blessed
them. Enlil declared that henceforth they "shall be like
unto us gods," and "reside far away, at the mouth of
the rivers."

Thus ends the Flood story within the Gilgamesh Epic.
Nothing is said in it about restocking the human race.
The epic itself continues by relating that Gilgamesh, following instruction, descended to the bottom of the sea
and obtained the thorny plant that bestows (eternal) life.
The name of the plant is "Man Becomes Young in Old
Age." While Gilgamesh was bathing in a pool that evening, a snake carried off the plant. Thus man failed to
obtain immortality.

This Babylonian Flood story differs in numerous details from the Sumerian one, but the differences are the
result of later expansion and adaptation. Enough similar
details remain to show that the Sumerian story is the ul-

timate source: a god reveals to a man, through the means
of a wall, that the gods have decided to send the Flood to
destroy mankind; there is concern to preserve "the seed"
("of mankind," Sumerian; "of all living things," Gilgamesh Epic); the god gives instructions by means of a
dream and the man builds a boat; windstorms cause the
Flood, which continues for seven days; then the man
opens a hatch on the boat; the man sacrifices to a god or
gods; the man becomes immortal, like the gods; the Sumerian names of two gods, Enlil and Anu, are preserved
unchanged.  Uta-Napishtim, "I found life," is a Babylonian translation of the Sumerian name Ziusudra, "he saw
life."

If we had the other two-thirds of the Sumerian story,
we undoubtedly would have more parallels.  The overall
pattern is the same, and the detail of the god giving revelation to the man by means of a wall is too specific and
too unusual to be accidental.  We do not have two independent stories here, but a Babylonian one ultimately dependent on the Sumerian.  The actual literary relationship
is indirect: from the Sumerian story to Atrahasis to the
Gilgamesh Epic.

## Babylonian Treatment of the Story

The kinds of alterations and additions made to the
Flood story as it was adapted to other cultures are important to observe.  Only thus can we understand its history.
This insight will be valuable when, in Chapter 6, we examine the Hebrew version in the Bible.  The first stage
in the process of adaptation was the Babylonian treatment of the Sumerian story.

While only farm animals were taken aboard in the Sumerian story, in the Babylonian versions birds and wild
creatures have been added.  In the Gilgamesh Epic "the
seed of all living things" is included, a major expansion.
Presumably this change would be the result of logical re-
flection, a recognition of the difficulty of explaining how

other living things happen to be here if only mankind and farm animals survived the Flood.

In the Sumerian account the scene is localized. The Flood destroys mankind by sweeping over the Sumerian cities, and in describing the founding of the cities, only five are named. The Babylonian accounts, however, do not list the cities, and "the seed of all living things" on the ship and the death of "all mankind" in the Flood clearly indicate that the Flood has become a universal one over the whole earth.

A shift in the very purpose of the story has taken place. The Sumerian story is very concerned with the promotion of religion and kingship. The hero who survived the Flood is a king; he is lauded as a reverent king who humbly obeys the gods; the story is preceded by the declaration that kingship has come down from heaven. These features are absent in the Babylonian accounts. In Atrahasis the hero is a king, but this aspect is not emphasized. In the Gilgamesh Epic Gilgamesh is a king, but neither this information nor anything else about kings is mentioned within the Flood story. In the latter, the Flood hero is not a king, but a wealthy citizen of the city of Shuruppak.

What was the purpose behind the version in Atrahasis? The beginning section must have been intended to explain how and why mankind was created: it was created to do the hard work! The purpose of the plague, droughts, and Flood features are less certain. Were they composed simply for entertainment? Are they intended to explain why such disasters occur? Are they intended to demonstrate convincingly the power of the gods? Perhaps all three motives were involved.

The poets who produced the Gilgamesh Epic used it for a different purpose. They were evidently attracted to the Flood story because its hero was rewarded with immortal life among the gods. By making a few changes and by composing a new framework, the poets used the story in an effort to explain why, unlike Uta-napishtim,

mankind cannot escape death. The cause of the Flood and
Enlil's previous attempts to diminish mankind were omitted, for they did not serve the poets' purpose.

The Sumerian account is not concerned with the moral nature of men or gods. In the Babylonian versions,
however, many of the gods were deeply distressed by the
mass murder of mankind; they wept, and the mother goddess especially laments the tragedy. In the Gilgamesh
Epic the god Ea criticizes Enlil for sending the Flood, and
remarks:

> On the sinner impose his sin,
> On the transgressor impose his transgression!
> (Yet) be lenient, lest he be cut off,
> Be patient, lest he be dis[lodged]!

This passage implies that the cause of the Flood is man's
sin. Thus in contrast to the Sumerian story and to the
story's framework in Gilgamesh Epic, the Babylonian
versions show some moral concern. This concern is expressed in two ways: man is regarded as a sinner,
and the gods condemn Enlil for his massacre of humanity.

On the other hand, in the Gilgamesh Epic the god Ea
is a liar on two separate occasions. He instructed Uta-
napishtim to deceive the people of the city so that they
would not save themselves, and when Enlil accused Ea
of revealing the gods' secret (that the Flood is coming),
Ea falsely denied his guilt and put the blame on Uta-napishtim's interpretation of the dream.


THE HURRIANS

The Hurrians were non-Semitic people (called "Hor-
ites" in Genesis) who migrated from Ararat (Armenia)
into northern Mesopotamia in the third millenium B.C.
Their origin in Armenia is indicated by the fact that the
Hurrian language is unrelated to any language except

Urartian, the language of ancient Armenia.  The Hurrians
were conquered by their neighbors to the northwest, the
Hittites, around 1370 B. C., and by the Assyrians in their
own midst around 1250 B. C.

The Hurrians in Mesopotamia learned Sumero-Baby-
lonian religion and culture from their southern neighbors,
the Babylonians.  Abundant evidence of this has come from
two border cities where the peoples and cultures met, Nuzi
and Mari.  At Nuzi archaeologists found thousands of clay
tablets written by Hurrian scribes, but in the Babylonian
language with some Hurrian words mixed in.  André Parrot directed the Louvre Museum's excavations at Mari
and found 20,000 cuneiform tablets in the palace library.
Although most of the tablets are inscribed in Old Babylonian, a few religious texts are written in Hurrian.  We
know from other evidence (see next chapter) that the Hurrians knew the story of the Flood.

In the Babylonian Flood story the mountain on which
the ark landed is Mount Nisir in the Zagros Mountains at
the eastern edge of Babylonia.  But in the Bible (Gen. 8:4)
the ark landed in "the mountains of Ararat," that is, the
mountains of Armenia.  Armenia, in what is now eastern
Turkey, is north of northern Mesopotamia.  The people
who made this change must have been familiar with Armenia.  The Hurrians came from Armenia, and their new
homeland adjoined it.  They were the earliest people who
knew both the Flood story and mountains of Armenia.
They must have changed the locale.  Thus the Hurrians
are an important link in the evolution of the story.


THE ASSYRIANS

Through the second millenium the Assyrians, located on the eastern side of north-central Mesopotamia, had
their ups and downs in trying to rule their region and
foreign lands.  Through the ninth to seventh centuries,
however,  they established an empire and ruled northern

Mesopotamia and often ruled Urartu (Armenia), Babylonia, Syria, and Palestine.

The Assyrians were interested in Babylonian and
Sumerian literature, and the educated read it. In his inscriptions Ashurbanipal reported his own experience:
"I, Ashurbanipal, learned the wisdom of Nabu [the patron
god of writing], the entire art of writing on clay tablets.
. . . I read the beautiful clay tablets from Sumer and the
obscure Akkadian writing which is hard to master."[17]

The Flood story traveled to Assyria too. This is
clearly shown by the Assyrian copies of it and by the
presence of both Babylonian and Assyrian copies in the
library of Ashurbanipal. That king personally knew the
story, for he mentions it in one of his inscriptions.[18]
The Assyrians can hardly be the people who changed the
landing place of the ark to Armenia, however, for they
were closer to Mount Nisir than to Armenia.

### The Assyrian Recension of <u>Atrahasis</u>

Only a few small fragments of an Assyrian version
or versions of Atrahasis have been found and translated.
What little is known supplies the following features.

When the people multiplied, Enlil could not sleep because of their noise. He convened the assembly of the
gods and persuaded them to send a plague on mankind.
Atrahasis urged Ea his lord to end the plague, which he
did. Then Enlil persuaded the gods to send a drought so
that people would starve to death. The situation became
so severe that families resorted to cannibalism.

In one fragment the god Ea revealed his message
to the reed hut. In two other fragments Ea instructed
Atrahasis on how to build a big boat. Atrahasis should
build it entirely of reeds, put a strong covering over it
for a roof, and caulk it with pitch. He should name the
boat "The Life Saver." Into it he should put barley, his
property, his wife and relatives, and the skilled workers.
He should also put in the boat the wild creatures of the

steppe that eat grass and the birds of the heavens; Ea
promised that he would send them to him and that they
would wait at his door.   Then Atrahasis remarked that
he had never built a boat, and he asked Ea to draw the
design on the ground.   In a fourth fragment Atrahasis
entered his boat and closed it.   The storm god Adad rode
on the four winds (the south, north, east, and west winds)
and produced a storm.   Other gods broke the dikes (and
made the canals overflow).   Zu with his talons rent the
heavens so that water poured out.   A mighty flood came
upon the peoples of the earth, and its noise made the
gods tremble.

In this Assyrian recension the main features of the
Babylonian Atrahasis  have been preserved, with only minor revisions.


## BEROSSUS

Although the Flood story spread to many lands and
cultures, it also continued to be popular in its homeland,
southern Mesopotamia.   Berossus, a Babylonian priest
of the god Marduk, lived in Babylon around 275 B.C.   He
wrote a history of Babylonia in Greek, using native documents as sources.   He included an account of the Flood.
His book has been lost, but Alexander Polyhistor (1st c.
A.D.) made an excerpt of his account of the Deluge, and
two summaries of that excerpt have survived.

The source(s) of the Flood story that Berossus used
preserved some ancient Sumerian aspects.   In Berossus'
account the hero's name, Xisuthros, is derived from the
Sumerian Ziusudra rather than from the Babylonian forms
Atrahasis and Uta-napishtim.   The Sumerian city, Sippar,
the city of the sun god, is honored as the keeper of
knowledge.

Berossus' account contains also some features of
the Babylonian versions。  For example, birds are included among the creatures taken aboard.   Unlike the

Babylonian accounts, in Berossus' version the boat landed in the Kurdish mountains of Armenia.

As in both the Sumerian story and in one or the other
of the Babylonian versions, the hero in Berossus is a
king.  He, too, offered sacrifice after the boat landed.
Because of his piety, he was rewarded with eternal life
among the gods, as were his wife, daughter, and boatman.

Berossus made a few alterations in the story to
adapt it to Greek readers.  The name of the Greek god,
"Kronos," has been substituted for Enki, or Ea.  The
dimensions of the boat are given in Greek "stadia" instead of Semitic "cubits."  The ark here is not a cube
as in the Gilgamesh Epic, but five stadia long and two
stadia wide (that is, more than 3000 feet by 1200 feet).
Berossus' account gives a particular date for the beginning of the Flood, namely, the fifteenth day of the
Macedonian month Daisios, a month which corresponds
with the Babylonian month Iyyar, the second month of
the year.

The importance of Berossus' version of the story
is threefold.  First, his account demonstrates that the
Flood story, with some ancient Sumerian features, was
still being retold in Babylon in 275 B.C.  Second, Berossus' Hellenizing of the story, that is, his substitu-
tion of some Greek terms for the earlier ones, illustrates the tendency of ancient writers to change stories to adapt them to new cultures.  Third, the landing site is moved northward, as in Genesis.

Thus this popular story moved northward, from
Sumer to Babylonia to northern Mesopotamia.  Along
the way it underwent changes as it was adapted to new
cultures and later eras.  The process continued as
the story turned westward.

# CHAPTER 5

## THE STORY MOVED WEST

The Flood story was too popular to stop at the northern boundary of Mesopotamia. It spread westward too, and found a place in many cultures.

## THE HURRIANS, HITTITES, AND CANAANITES

The Hurrians appear to have been the main carriers as the Deluge story moved west. In the second millenium B.C. they spread knowledge of Sumerian and Babylonian languages and literature to the Hittites. Excavators of the royal Hittite library at Boghazköy (in central Turkey) found thousands of clay tablets written in Hittite, Hurrian, and Babylonian. The Hurrians passed on to the Hittites both Babylonian and Hurrian literature. Fragments of the Flood story were found there too, in Babylonian, Hurrian, and Hittite languages.

The Hurrians brought Sumerian and Babylonian languages and literature as far west as the coast of Syria, for a bilingual Sumerian-Hurrian text and a bilingual Akkadian-Hurrian text have been found at Ras Shamra (the site of the ancient Canaanite city of Ugarit). Archaeologists believe that the alphabet of the Canaanites, the Ugaritic, is derived from the Akkadian (Old Babylonian) alphabet.

The Flood story reached the Canaanites too, for a fragment of a Babylonian version of it was found at Ras Shamra and published by J. Nougayrol. It is a brief account, written on one clay tablet, probably in the fourteenth century B.C. The orthography and grammar indicate that the tablet was inscribed in the West, but the text is based on a Babylonian account. On this fragment

the hero's name is Atrahasis, but, unlike the story Atrahasis, the Flood story is not preceded by a story of creation and Enlil's attempts to diminish mankind.  Unfortunately the small fragment preserves only the beginning
and end of the story. [19]

According to the fragment, after the great gods took
counsel, they "brought about a flood in the regions of the
world."  Atrahasis lived in the temple of his lord,  the
god Ea.  Ea repeated the decision of the gods to "the
wall, " which presumably (in the lost section of the tablet) passed on the information to Atrahasis.  The fragment concludes with the divine promise to Atrahasis that
he will have "life like the gods. "


## THE HEBREWS

As the story advanced to the west, it was appropriated by the Hebrews too, and was written down in their
language in the tenth century B. C.  Eventually it was incorporated into the Book of Genesis in their Scriptures,
where its literary form is prose instead of epic poetry.
Genesis 7:11 is poetic, however, and may be preserved
from an epic source. In  the next chapter we will discuss the story in Genesis in detail;  here we will ask
from what people the Hebrews learned it.

We are certain that the Hebrews did receive the story from their neighbors, because, as we shall see later,
the Hebrew and Mesopotamian Flood stories have far too
many features in common to have arisen independently.
And the Mesopotamian stories existed long before the
Hebrew, so the borrowing process has to be from the
Mesopotamian to the Hebrew, and not vice versa.

The earliest-known form of the Flood story, the
Sumerian account, stands as the ultimate source of the
biblical account.  The Sumerian story is not the direct
or immediate source, however, for the Hebrew version contains no features which are uniquely in the Su-

merian story.

Formerly biblical scholars believed that the Bible's source was a Babylonian account of the Flood. It is true that a fragment of the Gilgamesh Epic has been found at Megiddo in Israel.[20] A weakness of the Babylonian source theory, however, is that in the Gilgamesh Epic the mounttain that the ark lands on is Mount Nisir, whereas in the Bible the ark lands on "the mountains of Ararat." As we have seen, the Hurrians must have been the people who introduced that change in the locale. Unlike the Hurrians, the Hebrews never lived in "Ararat," so it is not a change that they would have made.

According to Genesis 11:31-12:6 Abraham's father Terah moved with his family from the city of Ur in Babylonia to the city of Haran, a major Hurrian center in northern Mesopotamia, and settled there. After Terah died at the age of 205 years, Abraham, acting on the Lord's command, moved with his family to the land of Canaan. A conservative view today is that Abraham carried the story from Ur to Haran to Canaan. This is very doubtful, for such a long migration is improbable, and the historical existence of Abraham has been seriously questioned in some recent studies. It is certain that others carried the story westward to Asia Minor and Syria, and they could have carried it to Palestine too. W. G. Lambert has suggested that this probably happened in the fourteenth century B. C.[21]

Everything considered, the Hurrian version seems to be the most probable source of the Hebrew Flood story. Commenting on the shift in Genesis away from Babylonian names, especially the change from Mount Nisir to the mountains of Ararat, Professor Speiser remarked that "Hebrew tradition must have received its material from some intermediate, and evidently northwesterly, source, and that it proceeded to adjust the data to its own needs and concepts."[22] The probability that the Hebrews learned the story from the Hurrians is increased by the fact that various other stories in Genesis reflect knowledge of customs and traditions that were peculiar to the Hurrians.[23]


## THE GREEKS AND ROMANS

Eventually the Flood story reached the Greeks. As Cassuto remarked, the Hittites probably were the people who transmitted it to them.[24] The Hittites ruled central Asia Minor, and the Greeks had colonies along the Asia Minor coast. In the fourth century B. C. the Greek philosophers Aristotle and Plato mentioned the Flood, which occurred in the days of Deucalion and Pyrra.[25] The Greeks made their share of changes in it to adapt it to their own culture.


### Apollodorus

Apollodorus, writing in Greek in the second century B. C., summarized the story very briefly. In another passage he referred to it by remarking that some people say that the cause of the Flood was "the impiety of Lycaon's sons." According to Apollodorus' summary, Prometheus advised his son Deucalion, who was king over part of Thessaly, to construct an ark. Deucalion built it, loaded it with provisions, and went aboard with his wife Pyrra. Then the mighty god Zeus sent a heavy rain, which "flooded the greater part of Greece, so that all men were destroyed, except a few who fled to the high mountains in the neighborhood." They floated in the boat for nine days and nine nights and drifted to Mount Parnassus. When the rain ceased, they landed on that mountain and Deucalion sacrificed to Zeus. Zeus sent Hermes to tell Deucalion to ask for what he wanted, and he chose to have more people again. Acting upon Zeus' advice, Deucalion and Pyrra picked up stones and threw them back over their heads. The stones which he threw became men, and the stones which she threw became women.

Although this Greek version is brief, it retains enough
of the Flood story's traditional elements to indicate that
its ultimate sources are the Mesopotamian accounts.
These features are the notion that the Flood was sent because of insufficient human reverence for the gods; the
hero is a king; a god advised the hero to build an ark,
which he loaded with supplies (but not animals and birds);
a god produced the Flood by means of heavy rain; a man
and wife survive in the ark, which lands on a mountain;
after landing, the hero sacrifices to a god; the usual concern for restocking the human race is expressed.   There
are too many similarities to be accidental.   The Greeks
did not take it from the Septuagint, the Greek translation (3d-2d c. B.C.) of the Old Testament, because the
word for ark in the Septuagint is kibōtos, whereas Apollodorus' term for the ark is larnax.

As usual, the Flood story underwent some changes
to adapt it to its new environment.   The gods and the survivors of the Flood have Greek names; the mountain is
in Greece; the method of creating more humans is Greek.

Ovid

The Greeks passed the story on to the Romans.   The
poet Ovid, writing in Latin in Rome at the close of the pre-
Christian era, has handed down to us  a  longer  account
based on the Greek story.   Some of the features in Ovid's
account are  readily  recognized  as  additions  from  the
Greek and Roman mythological background.

According to Ovid, Jupiter observed from his lofty
throne that mankind was not only  "contemptuous of the
gods," but also violent and murderous,  "greedy for
slaughter."   In anger he summoned a council of the gods
and declared that he must destroy the race of men, for
with their violence men threatened the safety of the demi-
gods on earth, that is, the deities of woods and fields:
the nymphs, fauns, and satyrs.   Jupiter reported to the
council that, disguised in human form, he had wandered

the earth to see if men were as bad as they had been reported to him.  When he gave a sign that he was a god,
the common people worshiped him, but king Lycaon had
mocked him.  Lycaon even killed a man, cooked his
flesh, and set it on the table before Jupiter.   Jupiter
hurled his thunderbolt; Lycaon ran and turned into a wolf,
"still delighting in slaughter. "  Jupiter reaffirmed to the
assembly that men all over the earth deserved to perish.

The gods were grieved when they heard this, and they
asked what would be the condition of the earth without mor-
tals, and who would bring incense to the altars of the gods.
Jupiter replied that they should be of good cheer, for "he
would give them another race of wondrous origin far different from the first. "

Jupiter considered hurling his thunderbolts at the
whole earth, but he feared lest this would destroy the universe by fire, as the fates had predicted would happen
sometime.  Instead, he let the South-wind loose, which
poured down rain.  He asked his sea-god brother, Triton
(Neptune), to produce large waves, and he told the rivers
to remove their restraining dikes and to loose their fountains.  Most men drowned; some died of slow starvation.

When Deucalion and his wife, carried in a little skiff,
landed on Mount Parnassus, the only land not covered by
the sea, they first worshiped the Corycian nymphs and
the mountain deities, and the goddess Themis, who kept
the oracles and revealed men's fate.  There was no better man than Deucalion,   "none more scrupulous of the
right. " No woman was more reverent of the gods than was
his wife.  Then Jupiter stopped the storm and, at his command, Triton blew his conch shell and made the waters
retreat.

Deucalion lamented to his wife that only the two of
them were left and that on them depended the human race.
He wished that he could restore the nations by breathing
the breath of life into molded clay, as his father Prometheus had done.  Deucalion and his wife wept, then went
to the shrine of the oracle goddess Themis and asked her

how their race might be restored.    She told them to go,
and "with veiled heads and loosened robes throw behind
you as you go the bones of your great mother." At first
they were dumbfounded by this command, because they
interpreted it literally.    Then Deucalion deduced that "the
bones" must be "the stones in the earth's body." So
they obeyed the order of the goddess, and the stones they
hurled assumed human form gradually.    The stones Deucalion threw became men, and those his wife threw became women.    The earth spontaneously produced the
other forms of animal life, for "when moisture and heat
unite, life is conceived."

In this Roman account the Greek features are generally retained and none added.    The change in the name of
the god from "Zeus" to "Jupiter" is, of course, a Roman adaptation.

In the Greek and Roman versions we find an emphasis on piety toward the gods as necessary. Ovid's account also regards men's violence and slaughter of each
other as utterly sinful.


## THE SYRIANS

When Lucian of Samosata described the Syrian city of
Hierapolis, he included a brief summary of the Flood story.  He lived in the second century A. D. , but the account
he summarized may have been current in Syria for centuries.  Although he wrote in Hellenistic Greek (because
it was still the prevailing language in the Near East), he
was not a Greek, and his account differs from the Greek
form of the story (in spite of his claim that he had learned
it from the Greeks).

Lucian described the sinful antediluvian men as "ex-
tremely violent" and "they neither kept oaths nor wel-
comed strangers nor spared suppliants." Only Deucalion
was saved from the Flood, because of his "prudence and
piety." When the earth gave forth much water, followed

by heavy rains, Deucalion with his children and wives
boarded a great "ark" (larnax) which he possessed. At
the same time horses, pigs, lions, snakes, and "every
kind of creature that grazes on earth came to him, all
of them in pairs." They did not harm him, because "from
some divine source, there was great friendship among
them." They floated together as long as the flood lasted
[the duration is not specified]. The inhabitants of Hierapolis claimed that a great chasm opened in their land and
took in all the flood waters (the Athenians had long claimed that the Flood waters had drained off through a cleft
in the ground in their territory).[26]

Lucian's account displays more parallels with the
Near Eastern versions than with the Greek. There are
at least seven parallels with Semitic sources.

1. Lucian stated that Deucalion was also called "Sisu-
thea," which probably is derived from the late Babylonian form (used by Berossus) of the ancient Sumerian name,
Xisuthros.

2. According to Lucian, "the earth gave forth much
water" and this, along with "heavy rains," caused the
Flood. This is somewhat parallel to Genesis 7:11, "all
the fountains of the great deep burst forth." The reference in both stories may be to springs.

3. In both Lucian and Genesis 7:19 we find the
clause, "the water(s) prevailed."

4. In Lucian's account, as in some Near Eastern
texts, including Genesis, more than just the man and
wife are saved from the Flood. In Lucian, "his children and his wives" are in the ark. Robert Oden specu-
lates that "his wives" means his wife and daughters-in-
law and that the passage is a parallel to Genesis 7:7.[27]
That interpretation is dubious, for there is no mention
of Deucalion's sons and daughters-in-law.

5. Pairs of animals were taken aboard. This feature is absent in the other versions of the story, except
in the P source used in Genesis 6:19-20.

6. Lucian's statement that "Deucalion alone of men"

remained is similar to "only Noah was left and those with
him in the ark" in Genesis 7:23.

7.  Lucian's remark that the human race  multiplied
from Deucalion (literally, "from Deucalion became -a
crowd") is like the Near Eastern versions of the story,
and unlike the  Greek version in which restocking the
race began by throwing rocks which changed to humans.
This reminds us somewhat of the command to Noah to
"multiply and fill the earth" in Genesis 9:1.

Although four of these parallels with the Near Eastern
versions of the story have some similarities to the Genesis accounts, it is apparent that the Septuagint was not a
direct source of Lucian's account, because there is too
much disagreement between it and Lucian within the parallels.  In each  parallel Lucian's Greek words and syn-
tax are different from those in the Septuagint, except number 3 above: "the water prevailed. "   Even  the Greek
term for ark is different; Lucian has <u>larnax</u> as in Apollodorus, not <u>kibōtos</u> as in the Septuagint.

Lucian's source probably was a Hellenistic version
which was current in Syria in the second century A. D. ,
a syncretistic account which mixed various Near Eastern features with the Greek version's name of the hero,
Deucalion, and its term for the ark, <u>larnax.</u>

## THE PHRYGIANS

In the late Hellenistic period, Apamea, a city in the
mountains of Phrygia in Asia Minor, apparently appropriated the Flood story from Jewish sources.  The citizens of Apamea consisted of many Jews along with the
gentiles.  They claimed that the ark landed there (see
chapter 8 below), and attached the label <u>Kibōtos</u> to the
name of their city.  <u>Kibōtos</u>, as we have noted, was the
Greek term for ark in the Jewish Septuagint.

Apamea continued for several centuries to connect
itself with Noah's ark.  During the reign of Emperor

Septimius Severus (A.D. 193-211), and later, the city
issued coins on which Noah's ark was represented.
Definite Jewish influence is manifest on those coins. (1)
On the ark the name "NŌE" is written in Greek, which
is the same form of the name as in the Septuagint. (2)
The ark, Noah, and his wife are portrayed in the Jewish
manner. Noah and his wife, appearing from the waist
upward, are standing in an open chest, or box; one dove
is perched on the raised lid of the ark, while another
dove flies toward it with a twig in its claws. To the left
is a second scene in which Noah and his wife are standing
on dry ground, holding up their right hands in adoration
of the Lord. (3) The two scenes are in the Jewish order:
from right to left. Hebrew and other Semitic languages
run in the opposite direction from European languages,
and the scenes in Jewish narrative art in the Roman
period did too. Of the two scenes on the coins, the one
on the left represents the later incident: Noah and his
wife are expressing their gratitude to God for their sal-
vation from the Flood. The same manner of portraying
Noah and the ark and the same order of the scenes (from
right to left) occurs in early Christian catacomb frescoes
at Rome. These particular frescoes, too, are derived
from Jewish art.

Thus the Flood story traveled in ancient times from
the deltas of the Tigris and Euphrates Rivers, up the
length of the Mesopotamian Valley, and westward to Asia
Minor, Syria, Palestine, Greece, and Rome. As the result of its being incorporated in the Bible, the story is
now known around the world, about 4500 years after its
birth in little Sumer.

Flood story, you have gone a long way, in both time
and space!

# CHAPTER 6

# THE STORY IN THE BIBLE

The Flood story in Genesis is more complex than the other Flood accounts. Unlike them, it contains significant contradictions and inconsistencies. Here are some examples.

## CONTRADICTIONS AND INCONSISTENCIES

> 1a. Then the Lord said to Noah,
> ". . . Take with you seven pairs of all
> clean animals, the male and his mate;
> and a pair of the animals that are not
> clean, the male and his mate; and seven
> pairs of the birds of the air also, male
> and female, to keep their kind alive upon
> the face of all the earth" (7:1a, 2-3).
> 1b. And God said to Noah, ". . .
> And of every living thing of all flesh, you
> shall bring two of every sort into the ark,
> to keep them alive with you; they shall
> be male and female. Of the birds accord-
> ing to their kinds, and of the animals ac-
> cording to their kinds, of every creeping
> thing of the ground according to its kind,
> two of every sort shall come in to you,
> to keep them alive" (6:13a, 19-20).

These two passages clearly disagree on the number of birds and of clean animals that should be taken aboard the ark (clean animals are those fit to eat; see Leviticus 11): seven pair in 1a, and one pair in 1b. The passages also disagree on the term for deity: "the Lord" vs. "God."

    2a.  And rain fell upon the earth forty days and forty nights. . . . At the end of forty days Noah opened the window of the ark which he had made, . . . He waited another seven days, . . . Then he waited another seven days (7:12; 8:6, 10a, 12a).

    2b.  In the six hundredth year of Noah's life, in the second month, on the seventeenth day of the month, on that day all the fountains of the great deep burst forth, and the windows of the heavens were opened. . . . In the six hundred and first year, in the first month, the first day of the month, the waters were dried from off the earth; . . . In the second month, on the twenty-seventh day of the month, the earth was dry. Then God said to Noah, "Go forth from the ark" (7:11; 8:13a, 14-16a).

These two sets of passages disagree on the duration of the Flood. In 2a a total of only 54 days (40 plus 7 plus 7) passed from the time that the Flood began until Noah left the ark. In 2b, however, the period was the equivalent of a solar year. The period appears to be more than a year (a year and ten days), but that is because time here is stated in terms of the old Near Eastern lunar year. [28]
    Biblical fundamentalists invariably either ignore these differences or try to interpret the verses to eliminate the differences and to harmonize the passages. Such procedure fails because it distorts the evidence. Either device--ignoring parts of the text or reinterpreting parts of the text--usually leads to misinterpretation of the text.

## THE DISCOVERY OF SOURCES

The only way to understand the cause of the inconsistencies is to recognize that we have before us an example of ancient composite literature. Two separate written sources have been conflated; that is, two sources, or extracts from two sources, have been interwoven into one account, without rewriting them to make their vocabulary, style, and ideas agree with each other. Conflation invariably produces contradictions and inconsistencies, and sometimes duplications. Ancient Near Eastern literature, including that of the Hebrews, often repeated ideas, however, so duplication of thought does not necessarily indicate several writers. On the other hand, duplication of an incident in a story is usually caused by conflation. Composite literature was very prevalent in the ancient world, and a major contribution of modern biblical scholarship is the recognition that much of both the Old Testament and the New Testament is composite.

The same two sources that are used in the Genesis Flood story run through the Pentateuch, where they are combined with other source material. The presence of written sources in the Creation accounts was first observed when H. B. Witter in 1711 recognized the significance of the different terms for God. Gradually biblical scholars discovered more and more evidence of earlier sources and later editing in the Pentateuch. The famous Graf-Wellhausen hypothesis assigned letters to the main sources: J, E, P, and D. Although the hypothesis has had to be revised and refined, it is basically sound. Orthodox Jews and Christians attack it because it upsets the traditional view that Moses wrote the Pentateuch, but the evidence for written sources is quite decisive. The contradictions, duplications, and linguistic inconsistencies cannot be sensibly explained as the composition of a single writer.

The passages quoted above in the "a" category (1a, 2a) are from the J source, in which the term for God is "the Lord." The passages in the "b" category are from the P source, in which the term is "God." J was written

in the tenth or possibly ninth century B.C., but the date
of P is sixth century and later -- P was written over a
period of time. J was a narrative document in which
stories were arranged in a chronological framework.
P was produced by Hebrew priests to promote their religion.

Duplication is another type of evidence that there are
two sources in the Genesis Flood story. Three instances
are quite plain. (1) Noah is told who and what to take
aboard (7:1-5, J; 6:18-22, P). (2) The Flood begins (7:10,
J; 7:11, P). (3) The deity promises not to do it again
(8:21-22, J; 9:8-11, P).

The evidence forms a pattern: the same passage that
is a duplication, or a contradiction, or causes a break
in the flow of thought, usually displays a difference in
vocabulary, especially the word for God.

If we are to understand the Flood story in the Bible
in relation to other Deluge stories, we must first separate it into its two accounts and let each speak for itself. The traditional practice of treating them as a single account, on the other hand, conceals the distinguishing characteristics of each, and presents a distorted picture of the Hebrews' treatment of the story.

Below is a reconstruction of the two sources, in the
Revised Standard Version, according to the analysis made
by Professor Speiser.[29] "R" indicates either an insertion made by a redactor (editor) or a later gloss made by
a scribe.


THE FLOOD STORY IN J

The Lord saw that the wickedness of
man was great in the earth, and that every
imagination of the thoughts of his heart was
only evil continually. And the Lord was
sorry that he had made man on the earth,
and it grieved him to his heart. So the

Lord said, "I will blot out man whom I
have created from the face of the ground,
man and beast and creeping things and
birds of the air, for I am sorry that I
have made them." But Noah found favor
in the eyes of the Lord (6:5-8).

Then the Lord said to Noah, "Go
into the ark, you and all your household,
for I have seen that you are righteous before me in this generation. Take with
you seven pairs of all clean animals, the
male and his mate; and a pair of the animals that are not clean, the male and
his mate; and seven pairs of the birds of
the air also, male and female, to keep
their kind alive upon the face of all the
earth. For in seven days I will send
rain upon the earth forty days and forty nights; and every living thing that I
have made I will blot out from the face
of the ground." And Noah did all that the
Lord had commanded him (7:1-5).

And Noah and his sons and his wife
and his sons' wives with him went into
the ark, to escape the waters of the flood.
Of clean animals, and of animals that are
not clean, and of birds, and of everything
that creeps on the ground, (two and two,
[R]) male and female, went into the ark
with Noah [R; Speiser overlooked this
gloss, suggested by 6:22 and 7:16]). And
after seven days the waters of the flood
came upon the earth (7:7-10).

And rain fell upon the earth forty
days and forty nights (7:12).

And the Lord shut him in. The flood
continued forty days upon the earth [Spei-
ser assigns part of this clause to P]; and

the waters increased, and bore up the
ark, and it rose high above the earth
(7:16c-17).

Everything on the dry land in whose
nostrils was the breath of life died. He
blotted out every living thing that was
upon the face of the ground, man and animals and creeping things and birds of
the air; they were blotted out from the
earth. Only Noah was left, and those
that were with him in the ark (7:22-23).

The rain from the heavens was re-
strained, and the waters receded from
the earth continually (8:2b-3a).

At the end of forty days Noah opened
the window of the ark which he had made,
and sent forth a raven; and it went to and
fro until the waters were dried up from
the earth. Then he sent forth a dove from
him, to see if the waters had subsided
from the face of the ground; but the dove
found no place to set her foot, and she
returned to him to the ark, for the waters were still on the face of the whole
earth. So he put forth his hand and took
her and brought her into the ark with him.
He waited another seven days, and again
he sent forth the dove out of the ark; and
the dove came back to him in the evening,
and lo, in her mouth a freshly plucked
olive leaf; so Noah knew that the waters
had subsided from the earth. Then he
waited another seven days, and sent
forth the dove; and she did not return
to him any more (8:6-12).

And Noah removed the covering of
the ark, and looked, and behold, the face
of the ground was dry (8:13b).

Then Noah built an altar to the Lord,
and took of every clean animal and of every
clean bird, and offered burnt offerings on
the altar. And when the Lord smelled the
pleasing odor, the Lord said in his heart,
"I will never again curse the ground because of man, for the imagination of man's
heart is evil from his youth; neither will
I ever again destroy every living creature
as I have done. While the earth remains,
seedtime and harvest, cold and heat, summer and winter, day and night, shall not
cease" (8:20-22).


## THE FLOOD STORY IN P

These are the generations of Noah.
(Noah was a righteous man, blameless in
his generation; Noah walked with God [R].)
And Noah had three sons, Shem, Ham, and
Japheth. Now the earth was corrupt in
God's sight, and the earth was filled with
violence. And God saw the earth, and behold, it was corrupt; for all flesh had cor-
rupted their way upon the earth. And God
said to Noah, "I have determined to make
an end of all flesh; for the earth is filled
with violence through them; behold, I will
destroy them with the earth. Make your-
self an ark of gopher wood; make rooms
in the ark, and cover it inside and out
with pitch. This is how you are to make
it: the length of the ark three hundred cubits, its breadth fifty cubits, and its
height thirty cubits. Make a roof [Speiser:
sky light] for the ark, and finish it to a cu-
bit above; and set the door of the ark in

its side; make it with lower, second, and
third decks. For behold, I will bring a
flood of waters upon the earth, to destroy
all flesh in which is the breath of life
from under heaven; everything that is on
the earth shall die. But I will establish my
covenant with you; and you shall come into the ark, you, your sons, your wife,
and your sons' wives with you. And of
every living thing of all flesh, you shall
bring two of every sort into the ark, to
keep them alive with you; they shall be
male and female. Of the birds according
to their kinds, and of the animals according to their kinds, of every creeping
thing of the ground according to its kind,
two of every sort shall come in to you to
keep them alive. Also take with you every
sort of food that is eaten, and store it up;
and it shall serve as food for you and for
them. " Noah did this; he did all that God
commanded him (6:9-22).

Noah was six hundred years old when
the flood of waters came upon the earth
(7:6).

In the six hundreth year of Noah's
life, in the second month, on the seventeenth day of the month, on that day all
the fountains of the great deep burst forth,
and the windows of the heavens were opened (7:11).

On the very same day Noah and his
sons, Shem and Ham and Japheth, and
Noah's wife and the three wives of his sons
with them entered the ark, they and every
beast according to its kind, and all the
cattle according to their kinds, and every
creeping thing that creeps on the earth

according to its kind, and every bird according to its kind, every bird of every sort. They went into the ark with Noah, two and two of all flesh in which there was the breath of life. And they that entered, male and female of all flesh, went in as God had commanded him (7:13-16b).

The waters prevailed and increased greatly upon the earth; and the ark floated on the face of the waters. And the waters prevailed so mightily upon the earth that all the high mountains under the whole heaven were covered; the waters prevailed above the mountains, covering them fifteen cubits deep. And all flesh died that moved upon the earth, birds, cattle, beasts, all swarming creatures that swarm upon the earth, and every man (7:18-21).

And the waters prevailed upon the earth a hundred and fifty days. But God remembered Noah and all the beasts and all the cattle that were with him in the ark. And God made a wind blow over the earth, and the waters subsided; the fountains of the deep and the windows of the heavens were closed (7:24-8:2a).

At the end of a hundred and fifty days the waters had abated; and in the seventh month, on the seventeenth day of the month, the ark came to rest upon the mountains of Ararat. And the waters continued to abate until the tenth month; in the tenth month, on the first day of the month, the tops of the mountains were seen (8:3b-5).

In the six hundred and first year, in the first month, the first day of the month, the waters were dried from off the earth

(8:13a).

In the second month, on the twenty-
seventh day of the month, the earth was dry.
Then God said to Noah, "Go forth from the
ark, you and your wife, your sons and your
sons' wives with you.  Bring forth with you
every living thing that is with you of all
flesh (birds and animals and every creeping thing that creeps on the earth [R;
Speiser assigns this to P]) that they may
breed abundantly on the earth, and be fruitful and multiply upon the earth."  So Noah
went forth, and his sons and his wife and
his sons' wives with him.  And every beast,
every creeping thing, and every bird, everything that moves upon the earth, went
forth by families out of the ark (8:14-19).

And God blessed Noah and his sons,
and said to them, "Be fruitful and multiply,
and fill the earth" (9:1).

Both the J and P accounts of the Flood begin with a
moral basis for it.  In J the Lord saw that mankind was
wicked and its thoughts were evil, whereas Noah was
righteous.  In P the earth was corrupt in God's sight
and filled with violence (the Hebrew term, chamas, can
mean simply "wickedness").

With the exception of one verse in P (8:16), both accounts list all the men ahead of all the women, as in "you
[Noah], your sons, your wife, and your sons' wives."
In P God blessed Noah and his sons, but none of the women; in the Gilgamesh Epic the god Enlil blessed the
hero and his wife.  Just how much of the preference
given men is caused by the interest in lineal descent
through the sons and how much is male chauvinism is an
open question.

Both J and P use the Hebrew word tebah as the term
for ark.  This word means "chest" or "box," and occurs

in Exodus 2:5 as the term for the basket in which the in-
fant Moses was placed.  Why was such a word used for
the ark instead of some word that meant "boat"?  The
only apparent reason is that the ark's shape, though not
its size, was that of a chest or box.


## CHARACTERISTICS OF J

Two of the most obvious features of J, which are not
in P, have been mentioned: "the Lord" as the name for
God, and the distinction between clean and unclean animals,
an old distinction in Hebrew and other religions.  Also the
numbers seven and forty are characteristic of J.  Seven
was a popular number in the Near East because of interest
in the seven planets and the seven days of the week.  "Forty days" occurs often in the Bible.  The Hebrew word ge-
shem, "heavy rain," is another linguistic feature of J's
Flood story.

In J, Noah sent forth birds after the rains ceased.
The ark apparently had no window, and in order to see that
the ground was dry, Noah had to remove the covering over
the ark.  Afterwards, Noah built an altar and offered up a
tremendous burnt offering, which consisted of some of every kind of clean animal and every kind of clean bird.  This
feature demonstrates that J's author or authors sought to
promote Hebrew ritualistic law.

It is interesting that J does not mention any landing
site for the ark.  Was this feature always absent in J, or
did the editors who combined it with E and P omit it?  If
J originally gave a landing location, was it the same as
in P?


## CHARACTERISTICS OF P

P's priestly authors were very much interested in
composing genealogies; therefore the term "genera-

tions" occurs often in P.    The word occurs in the Flood
story in Genesis 6:9.

Only P gives details of the ark's construction.    The
dimensions are given in Hebrew cubits: approximately
450 feet long,  75 feet wide,  and 45 feet high.

At first glance it may seem that the 150 days that
the Flood prevailed (7:24) is inconsistent with P's chronology of the Flood's duration of one (lunar) year and
eleven days.    Biblical scholars generally agree, however, that the 150 days is only the period while the Flood
was increasing; after that it gradually diminished.

It is P which gives a landing site for the ark: "the
mountains of Ararat."    As we have observed, this indicates some connection with the Hurrian version of the
Flood story.    Considering the late date of P, however,
its priestly writers may have learned of it indirectly
through some other group.

The covenant idea was very characteristic of Hebrew
religion.    Accordingly, the priestly writers interpreted
God's promise (not to send such a flood again) as a covenant between God and Noah and his descendants.    They
made the rainbow the sign of this covenant.

The situation after the Flood was similar to that after
the Creation: only a very few people were on earth to reproduce the human race.    Therefore the priestly writers
portrayed God as giving the same instruction in both sit-
uations.    He told Noah and his sons (9:1), as well as Adam
and Eve (1:28), "Be fruitful and multiply, and fill the
earth."    The same writers used the expression, "according to its kind," in both the Creation and Flood accounts
(1:25;  7:14).


## PARALLELS WITH OTHER FLOOD STORIES

The Flood accounts in both J and P contain these essential features of the Mesopotamian versions:
1.  A god becomes displeased with mankind.

2. Therefore the god decides to destroy all mankind, except one man and his wife or family, by means of a Flood.

3. A deity--either the same or a different god--warns the man that the Flood is coming; the god tells him to build a boat, and to put aboard himself, his wife, and some animals.

4. Storm or heavy rain is a major--and sometimes only--cause of the Flood.

The other Flood stories generally have these same features in common with each other too. Thus these elements were characteristic of the basic story.

### Mesopotamian Version

J has additional parallels with one or more of the Sumerian and Babylonian versions of the story. The exact day that the Flood will begin was predetermined; a special period of seven days preceded the Flood; one or more intervals of seven days occured at the end of the Flood; the hero opened a window or hatch at the end of the voyage; a covering for the ark is mentioned; a dove and a raven were sent out from the ark as the Flood neared its end, and the raven did not return. Berossus' account does not mention the species of birds, but, like J in Genesis, reports that they were sent out on three different days. Like Xisuthros in Berossus' account, Noah built an altar upon landing. In J, as in the Sumerian and Babylonian accounts, the hero offered a sacrifice after emerging from the ark. The Lord liked the smell of the burnt offering, as did the gods in general in the Gilgamesh Epic.

P, too, has parallels with one or more of the Mesopotamian accounts. The dimensions of the ark are given; the deity specifies its size, shape, and number of decks; pitch is used in its construction; the ark's door is mentioned; the ship lands on a mountain or mountains. After the Flood was over, the god Enlil blessed the hero and his wife in the Gilgamesh Epic, and God blessed Noah and his sons in P.

The word used for pitch is the same in P and in <u>Atraha-</u>
<u>sis</u>.  Especially strong evidence of direct influence on P
is the fact that elsewhere in the Old Testament, whenever
pitch is mentioned, one or the other of two different Hebrew words is used, rather than <u>kopher</u>, the word in the
Flood story.  This fact tells us that <u>kopher</u> was not in the
general Hebrew vocabulary and that the P writers must
have obtained it from their story source.

The Sumerian King List gives the names of the Sumerian kings who were supposed to have ruled before
the Flood.  In at least one form of it and in Berossus,
the last one is the tenth king and is the hero who survived the Deluge.  In P we find a list of ten patriarchs
who lived before the Flood, and the last one is Noah, who
also survived the Deluge.  Further, both the ten antediluvian kings and the ten antediluvian patriarchs lived to a
fantastic old age, which is even more exaggerated in the
Sumerian and Babylonian sources than in P.  In one Sumerian document Ziusudra had reigned for 36,000 years
before the Flood, while according to Berossus, Xisuthros lived for 64,800 years.  Noah was merely 600 when
the Flood started.  Although toned down considerably in
P, the old trait of exaggerating the age of the ancients
was still operating.

The large number of parallels demonstrates that
both the J and P Flood accounts are derived ultimately
from the Mesopotamian versions that preceded them.  An
interesting discovery is that J's parallels are generally
not in P, and vice versa.  This fact indicates that J's
source was not identical with P's source, which is not
surprising, considering that many forms of the story
were in circulation, and that P was incorporated in Genesis four or five centuries later than J.


HEBREW ADAPTATION OF THE STORY

Some of the Genesis changes and additions to the

Mesopotamian versions of the Flood story may have already been made in their sources.

One of the changes is in the duration of the Flood, which has been lengthened. In the Mesopotamian versions the Deluge usually lasted only seven days. In J, however, the duration is fifty-four days, and in P it is a solar year.

With the passage of time, the size of the ark grew tremendously. In the Gilgamesh Epic the length is 180 feet. In the P source in Genesis it is 450 feet--about half the length of a modern ocean liner. In Berossus the length is even more improbable: five stadia (3,030 feet). The Armenian version carried the idea the farthest; in it the ship is fifteen stadia long (9,090 feet). Tendency toward exaggeration is characteristic of the transmission of myths and folklore, and here there is an additional influence, namely, the desire to provide space for the numerous forms of life on board.

The shape of the ark is improved somewhat. Whereas the ark is a cube in the Gilgamesh Epic, in P it is 450 feet long, 75 feet wide, and 45 feet high. The rectangular shape continues in Berossus' account: five stadia by two stadia. The proportion of length to width, 6 to 1, of the Hebrew ark would produce a narrower ship than Berossus' 5 to 2. In the Gilgamesh Epic the ark has seven decks divided into nine compartments each; in P it has only three decks and an unspecified number of compartments.

No city is mentioned in Genesis, in contrast to the Mesopotamian accounts. Noah, unlike the earlier heroes, is not rewarded after the Flood with eternal life in the land of the gods. The divine announcement of the coming Deluge is received directly by Noah, not through a dream.

The trend was to expand the kinds of living creatures taken aboard. They increased from farm animals in the Sumerian story to all animals, birds, and creeping things in Genesis. Fish are not included, presumably because the Flood was no threat to them.

Other changes in the Flood tradition that we find in
Genesis were almost surely made by the Hebrews themselves.  These changes apparently are genuine adaptations by the Hebrews to their own culture, especially
their religion.

A change that has often been pointed out by historians is the obvious shift from polytheism to monotheism.
The assembly of the gods and mention of other gods have
been eliminated.  Only one god is involved, and he is
the Hebrew god, even though he is not called Yahweh in
the P account.  He is an omnipotent god in full control;
in contrast, one Mesopotamian god could thwart the plans
of another.  Although in general the shift to monotheism
in the ancient world was an improvement, it is possible
to become too enthusiastic about it, as some writers
have.  So much depends upon the concept of deity; the
character of the god or gods honored is more important
than the number.

Although in some other versions the hero of the
Flood is a king, in the Hebrew stories he is not.  This
change in the tradition is very understandable.  The Hebrews originally had no king.  After they settled in Canaan, they did not want one at first, but influenced by
the example of their neighbors, they reluctantly accepted a monarchy, beginning with Saul (around 1020 B.C.).
The Flood story probably entered Hebrew culture before
the time of David (around 1000 B.C.), when the kingship
became popular with the Hebrews.

Noah's name is a Hebrew contribution, and so are
the names of his sons in P.  The addition of the sons'
names appears minor in itself, but it is part of a large
plan to trace the ancestry of the priesthood, through Jacob, alleged father of Israel, back to Adam, the alleged father of mankind.  Through the device of genealogies, the priestly authors of P attempted to bolster
the prestige and authority of the Hebrew priesthood by
claiming that Aaron and his sons were descended from
Adam in a direct pure line unmarred by mixed mar-

riages. P's list of ten patriarchs, apparently suggested
by the Mesopotamian lists of ten prediluvian kings, provides the foundation.

The hero offered only an ox and a sheep in the Sumerian story, but in J the size of the sacrifice has been greatly enlarged. Noah offered "of every clean animal and of
every clean bird" (8:20). Noah's sacrifice was a burnt
offering, or whole offering, in which the whole animal or
bird was burnt up on the altar; according to Hebrew law,
this kind of sacrifice had to be male and ritually clean.
In the earlier versions of the Flood story, the sacrifice
was not a burnt offering. This change must have been introduced either by the Hebrews or by their northern
neighbors, for archaeologists have found evidence of this
type of sacrifice in ancient Canaan, Anatolia, and Greece,
but not in ancient Egypt or Mesopotamia.[30] Another Hebrew change in the tradition is that in J the sacrifice apparently is the cause of the Lord's vow that he will never
again destroy every living creature.

In J there is an upgrading of moral concern. Not only man's deeds, but "the thoughts of his heart" are judged
and found to be wicked. This is a more discerning basis
for morality than deeds alone, for thoughts involve motives. Even deeds alone form a higher basis than we find
in the Sumerian account, where, for mere piety, the hero
is rewarded with immortality. The Hebrews did not dis-
card the piety theme, however, especially in J where Noah offers a huge sacrifice.

On the other hand, God is not condemned in Genesis
for his wholesale destruction of mankind, in contrast to
the Babylonian versions in which the god Enlil is called
to task for his unthinking destruction of the people. The
Bible lacks any explicit statement of divine remorse for
the Flood. Nevertheless, divine regret seems to be im-
plied by the vow not to repeat the Flood. A parallel with
the Gilgamesh Epic supports this interpretation. When
Ishtar was about to rebuke Enlil for his cruel deed,

> She lifted up the great jewels which Anu
>           had fashioned to her liking:
> "You gods here, as surely as this lapis
> Upon my neck I shall not forget,
> I shall be mindful of these days, forget-
>           ting (them) never."

Thus Ishtar vowed by her lapis lazuli jewels that she would not forget the Flood. In P, God makes an everlasting covenant (which could be a Hebrew adaptation of the idea of the vow) with Noah and his sons and with every living creature on earth (9:8-11, 17) not to send a flood again. The sign of his covenant is the bright rainbow, even as bright blue jewels were the symbol of Ishtar's vow. Ishtar will "not forget" these days, and God will "remember" his covenant (9:16).

## GREEK, ROMAN, AND SYRIAN VERSIONS

The Greek and Roman versions of the Flood story have been changed yet further away from the Mesopotamian accounts. This is in harmony with the fact that they were written later than the two Hebrew stories and the added fact that they have been adapted to other cultures. Nevertheless, a few parallels between them and the Genesis stories remain, as we have seen. Lucian's Syrian account has more elements in common with the biblical versions. Lucian probably used a Hellenistic source which combined elements from the Hebrew and non-Hebrew accounts.

## CHAPTER 7

## DID THE FLOOD EVER OCCUR?

Now that we have traced the history of the Flood story up to the beginning of the Christian era, we are ready to ask: Did the Flood ever happen? Is the story based on an actual Flood?

## GEOLOGY AS EVIDENCE

They who are eager to prove the historicity of the biblical account of the Flood have often tried to use geology as evidence. The first man known to use a geological argument for the Deluge was Tertullian, a church father in Carthage around A.D. 200. He regarded the presence of marine shells in the rocks on mountains as proof that the Flood had occurred. [31] He did not know, as geologists do today, that the mountains were formed after the shells were deposited on the bed of the sea. It is not surprising, however, that in an era before geological science existed, Tertullian thought that marine shells on a mountain indicated that the sea had risen to that height.

In the seventeenth century several writers in Italy and England concluded that the fossils, bones, shells, and the strata in rock formations must have been produced by the biblical Flood. Some other writers opposed them on the ground that rock fossils could not be left by living things; admittedly, that was not a valid objection, for fossils do indeed result from living things. Nevertheless, the fossils, bones, shells, and strata are not evidence of a Flood, for they are the result of natural geological forces acting over a period of millions of years.

In the eighteenth century the Deluge was generally accepted as the cause of the condition of the earth's crust, with its fossils and strata.  Coal was recognized as a sedimentary deposit of organic material and was thought to be evidence in support of the Flood theory.

Nevertheless, a few men contended that so many layers of sedimentary deposits could not possibly have occurred in such a brief time.  They advocated the theory of uniformity, which maintains that natural forces operate in a uniform manner, in any age, and therefore the geological process of forming strata was a slow process in the past just as it is in modern times.  In opposition to the theory of uniformity, the apologists for the Flood proposed a theory of their own: the theory of "catastrophism."  According to this notion, God speeded up the geological processes enormously during the catastrophe of the Flood.

In the nineteenth century, churchmen in Europe and America lost control of education, and scientists conducted geological research.  The result of these two factors was that the theory of uniformity gradually replaced the Flood as the explanation of geological phenomena.  According to it, there have been many catastrophic floods, and the biblical Flood was merely the last one.  Later Louis Agassiz, a founder of the scientific study of glaciers, demonstrated that some gravel deposits were formed by glaciers, not floods.  Throughout the nineteenth century many apologists tried to defend the faith in the Flood, in opposition to the growth of geological knowledge and the rise of the theory of evolution, both of which discredited the Flood and the Creation stories.

At the beginning of the twentieth century George F. Wright offered a new rationalization of how the Flood could have occurred.  He proposed that at the end of the Ice Age the glaciers melted so fast that they caused a universal Flood.  This and some of the other suggestions ignore the fact that, in the Flood story, rain is the main cause, except that in the P source in Genesis, the water came also from "the great deep."

After surveying the history of "Deluge geology," by

which writers tried to reconcile the Flood story with geological evidence, Byron Nelson regretfully admitted that Deluge geology has been eclipsed by "modern geology." He blamed this state of affairs, not on the evidence, but on a disregard for God and the Bible.[32] At the end of his survey, Nelson abandoned hope of establishing the Flood theory through evidence; to believe in the possibility of the Deluge, he wrote, "one must <u>know</u> <u>God.</u>"[33]

The widespread existence of sedimentary deposits is still used by fundamentalists as an argument for the Flood. The argument is worthless for many reasons. First, no set of deposits around the world appears to have been caused by a universal Flood. Second, the argument overlooks the fact that there have been many other causes of sedimentary deposits besides floods: deposits on ocean floors which subsequently were raised and became dry land (for example, western Oregon and Washington); deposits in lake beds; alluvial deposits in river deltas. Instead of admitting this, fundamentalists generally ignore the real causes and assume that all deposits were made by the Flood. Third, the various deposits did not occur at the same time, but the Flood zealots usually assume that they did. Fourth, the causes of the deposits operated far too slowly to fit the story of Noah. Fifth, most of the deposits were formed before mankind existed.

The presence of fossils in the rocks, too, are still used--without sensible reason--as an argument to support the Flood story. The five reasons given above against the sedimentary deposits argument apply also to the argument based on fossils. Fossils, as well as sedimentary deposits, were formed over millions of years, not in forty days, or a year, or even one person's lifetime. Most of the supporters of the Flood ignore this evidence. They also overlook the fact that fossils and sedimentary deposits are generally far below the level where human bones are found, which shows that mankind appeared on earth much later than those formations. And

if the fossils generally result from one Flood, why are
there not generally human skeletons in the same strata ?
Or, if some of the fossils are not from one great Flood,
why should we think that any are ?    Flood enthusiasts
also fail to mention that the fossils were formed millions
of years earlier than the period assigned to the biblical
Flood.

An amazing feature of the Flood apologetics is the
effort to use sea shells and fish fossils as evidence to
support the historicity of the story.  Fish fossils in sedimentary rock have been claimed as evidence that they
died in the Deluge.  But would the Flood kill fish ?  The
ancient writers did not think so, for none of the Flood
stories state that fish were taken aboard the ark to save
them.  Actually, the fact that the majority of the fossils
are from creatures that lived in the sea demonstrates
that fossils are not reliable evidence for the biblical
story.

Geology not only tells us that there has been no
universal Flood during the age of mankind, but it demonstrates clearly that the earth is billions of years old,
not just a few thousand as biblical chronology would make
it.  According to geological evidence, some forms of in-
vertebrate life have existed here for more than 500 million years.  Geology further shows that even mankind has
been here far longer than literal acceptance of Genesis
would lead us to believe--millions, not thousands, of
years.

Local Flood Theory

Another type of geological argument is the local
flood theory, that is, the theory that the Flood account
in Genesis is based on an actual flood, but that flood
was only a local one in Mesopotamia.  As early as 1839
John Pye Smith in England observed the lack of geological evidence of a universal Flood.  He concluded that the
Flood must have been a local one in the Mesopotamian

Valley. What he observed when geological science was in its infancy remains true today: there is no geological evidence of a global Flood. But whether the Deluge story is based on a particular inundation is another question.

In the 1920s Sir Leonard Woolley, Stephen Langdon, and others excavated the sites in lower Mesopotamia. Woolley and Langdon found a layer of clay deposited by river floods at Ur and Kish, respectively. They assumed that both alluvial deposits were from the same flood. Although they recognized that the flooding was only local, they enthusiastically declared that it must have been the flood reported in the Bible. Archaeologists realized later, however, that there were several floods at Kish, all in the third millenium B.C., whereas the one at Ur was in the fourth millenium B.C. Obviously, it was not the same flood at both cities. Thus the floods were quite local, for none covered the whole of southern Mesopotamia. In fact, the flood at Ur did not even cover the whole town, for excavations in some sections of Ur disclosed no alluvial deposits. Evidence of local floods has been found at other Meospotamian cities, including Shuruppak, Uruk, Lagash, and Nineveh, all in the third millenium. All of these floods were only local river floods, for no marine shells or marine fossils were found. Furthermore, excavators at Kish found, below the flood deposit there, some cylinder impressions representing Gilgamesh. This discovery indicates that the Gilgamesh story in the Gilgamesh Epic existed before the floods at Kish. [33a]

André Parrot, in his book on the Flood, modified the local flood theory by suggesting that, although there were numerous local floods in the Mesopotamian region, one must have been so impressive that it inspired the Flood story. This theory is generally rejected today, for none of the Mesopotamian floods appear to have been so tremendous.

EARTH'S TILT

In 1820 Thomas Rodd defended the historicity of the
Deluge in his book, A Defense of the Veracity of Moses.
In it he set forth an ingenious, but worthless, explanation
of how the Flood supposedly happened.  He based his theory on the fact that the axis on which the earth rotates is
not perpendicular to its orbit, but tilted at an angle of
twenty-three and a half degrees.  Rodd boldly declared
that originally the axis must have been perpendicular,
but God suddenly changed the tilt, which caused the seas
to flood all the land.

Balsiger and Sellier mention a revised version of
that old theory.  According to it, the earth's axis suddenly changed 2345 B.C. [approximately the date set for
the Flood by Archbishop Ussher] from nearly vertical to
an inclination of twenty-six and a half degrees; after
that, it changed gradually by A.D. 1850 to its present tilt
of twenty-three and half degrees. [34]  The sudden shift in
2345 B.C. caused the Flood!  Balsiger and Sellier do not
necessarily accept the theory in their book, but in the
film, "In Search of Noah's Ark," the theory was presented as a modern theory in astronomy, a theory which
supports the belief that the Flood happened and "the Bible is true."  According to the film, the sudden change
in the earth's tilt could have occurred in the time of Noah.

There is no solid evidence that a sudden change in
the earth's inclination ever occurred.  The whole alleged
argument from astronomy is nonsense.

ARCHAEOLOGY AS EVIDENCE

Although they have excavated to great depths in many
places, archaeologists have never found evidence that at
any time since mankind has been on earth has there been
a universal Flood.  If there ever had been such a Deluge,
it would have left its mark everywhere at the same time.

Many ancient towns underwent no floods at all. They include the numerous towns excavated in Palestine and Syria, which are among the oldest in the world. Excavations at Jericho, for example, have revealed that the city existed nine thousand years ago, yet archaeologists found no sign of any flood there throughout its history.

Fundamentalists usually accept Archbishop James Ussher's biblical chronology, which he published in 1650-54. He calculated the date of the Flood as 2348 B.C., which happens to be the beginning of the Sixth Dynasty in Egypt. The tomb autobiographies of the nobles of that period mention no such Flood, and they are full of confidence and serenity, which would hardly be the case if the land were recovering from such a disaster. In fact, there would not be any people there at all!

If Noah's Flood had really happened, there would be a long period in each country when there would be no or few people living. No matter how fertile Noah's descendants were, restocking the human population, even in the Near East alone, would take time--a lot of time! On the contrary, the records of the Egyptian tombs and temples show that human civilization went on in Egypt continuously from 3000 B.C. to Roman times. There is no gap in Egyptian, Indian, Palestinian, or Syrian history resulting from a complete elimination of the human population.

Balsiger and Sellier try to use artifacts found in rock as evidence for a universal Flood. [35] They overlook the possible causes other than the Flood. They present as evidence a metal bowl found in conglomerate rock in Massachusetts. Conglomerate rock is formed by glaciers and by rivers, and a far more reasonable explanation of the bowl in the conglomerate is that someone dropped or threw it into a river, and in time it was covered by rock and sand deposits.

## THE WATER PROBLEM

One of the many difficulties confronting the eager believers of the Flood story is the water problem. Since there is not enough water on the earth to cover it all to a depth sufficient to reach the tops of the mountains, the question arises, From what source could all the water come? Rain cannot be the answer, for there is not that much water in the clouds. The moisture in the clouds has evaporated from the surface of the earth. It is not additional water, but merely water that is being "recycled." Furthermore, a continuous rainfall over the whole earth for forty days and forty nights is impossible, for the clouds do not store that much water. The moisture in the air around the earth would have to be "restocked" by more evaporation long before the fortieth day.

As usual, the defenders of the Flood resort to wild speculation. The basic tenet in their imaginative solution to the water problem is that the physical condition of the earth must have been radically different from its nature today. One theory is that before the Deluge there must have been a permanent cloud cover, a "water vapor canopy," around the whole earth; this canopy presumably would contain enough moisture to make possible a global heavy rainfall for forty days.

A further ingenious notion to account for a larger water supply before the Flood is the theory of subterranean reservoirs. According to this idea, there must have been vast bodies of water under the earth's surface, and these were released when the Flood began. This notion is suggested by the statement that "all the fountains of the great deep burst forth" in Genesis 7:11. As we have already observed, this remark in Genesis was based on the mistaken belief that the earth is flat and a body of water is below it; the water is under pressure, and bursts forth as springs when released.

A different approach to the water problem is to theorize that the earth suddenly became more level so that

less water was required to cover it.   Thus the floor of
the seas rose and continents sank.

But what would cause the water vapor canopy to turn
suddenly to rain, and/or the subterranean reservoirs suddenly to burst forth, and/or the sea floors to rise and the
mountains to sink ?  In this age of religious pseudo-sci-
ence, the Flood zealots have some imaginative answers.
Maybe a small planet flew by and upset the gravitational
balance, or maybe a gigantic meteorite collided with the
earth, or maybe . . .  [If so, why is that stupendous
event not mentioned in the Bible ?]

And after the Flood, where did all the water go ?
That is a tremendous problem too, but so far the Flood
enthusiasts seem to be much more interested in where
the water came from than where it all went.


THE MEMORY ARGUMENT

In addition to the Sumerian Flood story and its descendants that we have traced, various other flood stories
were known to ancient peoples.   Many are reported in Sir
James Frazer's classic work, Folklore in the Old Testament.  The Iranians, Chinese, Melanesians, and American
Indians had legends of some sort of a flood.   But as Cassuto recognized, [36] they are too divergent from the biblical
story to have a literary connection with it or its Near Eastern sources.   Thus this group of flood stories arose independently, in distinction to the group we have been examining, which is ultimately derived from the Sumerian story.

The memory argument is that flood legends were so
widespread in the ancient world that they must be the result of the transmission, through generation after generation, of a memory of a common event in the remote past.

The argument is not valid, for several reasons.

1. As folklorists and historians know, the existence
of a certain type of story among many primitive peoples
invariably is not the result of memory of a single, com-

mon event.  In fact, no example of such an event is known.
Instead, some types of stories were prevalent because
some feature was common in various environments.  Man
peoples told stories of floods because floods occurred in
their regions.  Many cultures had stories about mountains
because there were mountains in their lands.  Also, some
types of stories were widespread because of common human psychology.  Primitive cultures usually have creation
stories;  the cause is not a common memory of an act of
creation, but a common psychological curiosity of how
life began.  As Sir William R. Halliday expressed it in
his article, "Folklore": "Many of the general ideas which
find expression in popular customs and superstitions are
doubtless the product of simple psychological reactions to
environment, which are common to human nature in all
parts of the world, . . ."[37]  An analogy to the memory
theory of the Flood is Max Müller's theory of folklore
which he advocated a century ago.  He proposed that the
folktales and customs common to all European countries
must be derived from a single source, a primitive Aryan
culture.  E. B. Tylor and Sir James Frazer, however,
exposed the fallacy of that theory by showing that similar
but unrelated tales and customs had arisen independently
in primitive societies all over the world. [38]

2.  The flood stories that have no literary connection
with the Mesopotamian Flood story vary from each other
so much that independent origin is far more probable than
derivation from a common event.  If they represent memory of a single event, then memory is not reliable, for
the stories vary tremendously from each other.

3.  The flood stories are much too mythological to
be based on memory of an actual event.  Gods and goddess
es invariably play key roles in them, and this feature is
characteristic of folktales, not of human events.

4.  No "memory" of a universal Flood exists in some
ancient civilizations, as for example in Egypt.  M. S. and
J. L. Miller have stated the situation concisely: "Flood
stories are frequent in the ancient literature of many of th

world's peoples.  Efforts to link them all together as evidence of one universal event in which all life suffered are , however, futile.  Egypt, where the annual flooding of the Nile is considered a blessing, has no such catastrophic legends. [39]

5.  John Bright accepted the memory theory, but he knew that archaeology provides no evidence of such a universal catastrophe.  Therefore he set the date of the Flood in the early Stone Age, [40]  earlier than archaeology can trace.  This theory, however, is founded on rationalization, not on evidence.  Nevertheless, geology can trace back that far, and finds no evidence of a universal Flood in the Stone Age.

## ARK ON ARARAT ARGUMENT

To understand the current zeal to find the ark on Mount Ararat, we must recognize it for what it is: another argument intended to support the faith that the Flood occurred and the "Bible is true."  The zeal springs from that motivation, not from evidence.  We will postpone discussion of this argument until the next section of the book.

## IMPLAUSIBILITY OF THE STORY

All versions of the Flood story are so full of improbable elements that the story cannot possibly be history.  The only version believed today is the conflated one in Genesis, and it would not be believed, even by the few, if it were not in the Bible.  Is it at all possible that such a Flood as that described in the Bible could really have happened?  The numerous implausible features induced Jews and Christians long ago to try to explain them.  Philo, the rabbis cited in the Talmud, and Augustine all struggled with the problem.  The Christian Apelles, writing around A.D.

130, ridiculed the notion that an ark would have space for
so many animals and their food for a year. [41] In the third
century A. D. the pagan Celsus regarded the story of an
ark containing specimens of all living things as a story
"merely for young children. "[42]

Hermann Gunkel once called attention to the implau-
sibility of anyone's knowing God's secret thoughts (Gen.
6:5-8) or the depth of the Flood (7:20).

> The question how the reporter could know of
> the things which he relates cannot be raised
> in most cases without exciting laughter.  How
> does the reporter of the Deluge pretend to know
> the depth of the water ?  Are we to suppose that
> Noah took soundings ?  How is anyone supposed
> to know what God said or thought [either] alone
> or in the councils of Heaven ?[43]

Furthermore, how could anyone have observed that
the rain and the Flood were over the whole earth or that
"all the high mountains under the whole heaven were covered" (7:19) ?  In fact, there was much of the earth that
ancient man did not know existed; he thought that the
world was flat.

Another absurd feature of the traditional belief that
Noah put aboard two (or more) of every kind of animal,
bird, and reptile is that many did not exist in his region.
Since Noah did not have time to round up creatures from
all over the world, pairs of them would have to come to
him from Africa, Siberia, Alaska, Australia, etc.  John
Pye Smith raised this objection to the historicity of the
story in 1839, and Robert Jamieson developed it in 1870.
Jamieson remarked on the difficulties the animals would
have as those from polar regions and torrid zones suddenly migrated to a temperate zone. [44]  Marcus Dods,
in his commentary on Genesis in The Expositor's Bible,
observed that the animals in far-away places would have
had to select two of their number to be saved.  Then these

pairs would have to start months in advance and cross thousands of miles of sea and find Noah by "some inscrutable instinct."[45] Of course, fundamentalism's answer is miracles: "with God, everything is possible."

Many have remarked that there were far too many species of animals to get them all into any ark. Even more space would be required for the provisions necessary to feed such a menagerie for a year. The ancient world was not capable of building such an enormous boat.

In addition to the task of getting all those animals aboard, there would be the even greater problem of caring for them for forty days (J) or for a year (P). Various writers have pointed out that there were not enough people present to carry food to them or clean out their stalls. Whitcomb and Morris have postulated a novel solution: all the animals hibernated![46]

And what would the carnivorous animals eat? Other animals on the ark? I once saw a cartoon--don't recall where--in which there are only two animals left on the ark: a lion and a dog. The lion looks at the dog and says, "I'm still hungry."

Noah's sacrifice of some of every kind of clean animal and clean bird in the J account (8:20) is utterly implausible because of the tremendous size of such a sacrifice and the ridiculous wastefulness at a time when there was such a great need to restock the earth.

We have already observed that there simply was not enough water in the world for rain to pour for forty days and nights or for the Flood to cover all the mountains on earth.

Noah's age of 600 years at the time of the Flood, followed by his living to a total age of 950 years, is another impossibility.

Not least among the implausible elements is the feature that God, or a god, would deliberately kill off nearly all life on earth, including mankind.

STORY OR HISTORY ?

When the Genesis Flood is traced back to its ultimate sources, which are the Sumerian story and the Babylonian versions of it, those sources very clearly are fictional. The sources are poetry, composed and transmitted for entertainment and to promote various ideas. Again we quote Gunkel.

> Moreover, it should not be forgotten that many of the legends of the Old Testament are not only similar to those of other nations, but are actually related to them by origin and nature. Now we cannot regard the story of the Deluge in Genesis as history and that of the Babylonians as legend; in fact, the account of the Deluge in Genesis is a younger version of the Babylonian legend. [47]

The differences between the Hebrew versions and the Mesopotamian versions are not at all an indication that the Hebrew accounts are independent in origin. Josephus, writing in the first century of the Christian era, clearly illustrates for us the ease with which Jews (and others) readily appropriated and reinterpreted foreign material. In his treatise Against Apion he comments on Berossus' account:

> This author, following the most ancient records, has, like Moses, described the Flood and the destruction of mankind thereby, and told of the ark in which Noah, the founder of our race, was saved when it landed on the heights of the mountains of Armenia (I. 128-30).

In Berossus' account the name of the man who was saved by a boat he built is Xisuthros; Josephus conveniently ignores this fact and claims that Berossus was writing about Noah. Josephus deliberately overlooked the Babylonian setting of Berossus' story, including the detail that the hero was a king of Babylon, not a Hebrew patriarch. Josephus, like his ancestors, did not hesitate to Hebrewize the Flood story by adapting it to Hebrew tradition.

If someone wants to defend the old view that the story must be true because God revealed it through divine inspiration to Moses, let him explain why there are contradictions within the story itself in Genesis. If his answer is that man is responsible for the contradictions, maybe he should consider the possibility that man is responsible for the whole story. Also, if the source is divine inspiration, why did God use a different word for "pitch" in the Flood story than he did in the rest of the Old Testament? And why is some of the other vocabulary different in the Flood story? The use of a written source for the Flood story is a sensible explanation; the theory that God changed his diction to Moses when he was dictating that portion of the Old Testament is not.

The numerous implausible elements, not only in the Genesis account, but in all versions of the Flood story, tell us plainly that we are in the realm of fiction, not history.

The prominence of the mythological features demonstrates that the story is indeed a myth, not a report or even a faint "memory" of an historical event.

If the Flood is historical, why is there no archaeological or geological evidence of a universal Flood?

In short, the Flood story is simply that--a story, not history. If we are to be fair to it, we must accept it on its own terms, as a story.


## VALUE OF THE STORY

What is the importance of the Flood, as a story, for us? What does it offer to modern mankind?

Looking at it historically, the story contributes know-

ledge and understanding of the ancient world. It reveals
some of the thought and customs of the people. The Mesopotamian versions show the prominence of kings in the
culture. The Hebrew versions demonstrate a shift away
from the emphasis on kingship, which is replaced by emphasis on legendary patriarchs. The Greek and Roman
stories reflect Greek and Roman mythology and thought.

Looking at it from a literary standpoint, the story
provides much insight into ancient literature and its transmission. It illustrates the variety of forms a story could
take: epic poetry, song, and narrative. It is especially
important as an illustration of the process of adaptation
when a story was transmitted from one culture to another.
The various versions demonstrate that differences among
stories do not necessarily mean that the stories were independent in origin. Rather, when the stories have significant features in common, those features indicate that
we have different adaptations of the same story, not different stories.

Even in the twentieth century, the Flood remains an
entertaining story. Children are fascinated by the notion
of a family saving itself and all kinds of animal life by
floating on an ark.

Looking at the story from the standpoint of religion
and ethics, what is its value today ? In the Mesopotamian
versions, the moral concern is only that some deities
weep over the enormous loss of life; the Flood does not
have a moral cause, for mankind's faults are merely
that it is too numerous and too noisy. In the Hebrew and
Roman versions, however, the Flood is the result of
mankind's wickedness; clearly these versions teach that
evil is wrong and people should not engage in it. In the
P account in Genesis God sent the Flood because "all
flesh" (animals too ?) was corrupt and the earth was
filled with violence. In Ovid's version written for the
Romans, the Flood has a moral cause too: mankind is
violent and murderous, "greedy for slaughter." Thus
violence is first mentioned in the later Hebrew version,

and in the Roman account is one of the two sins (the other is impiety). This suggests that in the Mediterranean world there was a developing opposition to murder and war as a way of life. The J account in Genesis adds the essential ethical principle that wicked thoughts as well as wicked deeds should be eliminated. Thus the Greek and especially the Hebrew versions of the story are concerned with establishing a moral society. The moral lesson is taught just as effectively in the form of a story, as it would be by a report of a historical event. Nevertheless, all forms of the story are weak in regard to the moral responsibility of the gods for destroying so much life, human and otherwise.

Some versions of the story try to teach the necessity of piety toward the gods. In the Sumerian version, the hero apparently was selected to be saved because he faithfully worshiped the gods, and in Ovid's account, one of the two causes of the Flood was that mankind was "contemptuous of the gods." A weakness of many religions throughout history is that they have taught that the gods were proud, vain, and selfish, demanding constant praise, prayers, and gifts--a teaching actively fostered by the priesthood, which had a vested interest in piety. In the Hebrew versions of the story, however, piety is not even mentioned, except in a redactor's insertion. Thus the biblical versions of the Flood, by making man's moral deeds and thoughts the basis of judgment, rather than his piety, are superior to the other versions of the story and even to many parts of the Bible, including parts of Genesis.


## EFFECTS OF BELIEVING THE STORY IS TRUE

According to fundamentalism, the belief that the Flood story is "true" results in a higher quality of religion than does the belief that it is simply a story. But that is not the case at all! Belief that the Flood was an

actual event produces an inferior type of religion, for
several reasons.

First, as we have seen, all the evidence indicates
that the Flood never happened.  The many implausible
elements in the story, the archaeological and geological
evidence against the occurrence of a Flood over the
whole earth, and the nature of the origin of the story--
these collectively provide abundant evidence that the
story does not report actual history.  If we insist, however, that belief in its being a "true" story is vital for
religion, then we make credulity an essential element
in faith.  Why have a religion that makes virtues out of
credulity and ignorance ?  That is surely not a very high
level of religion!

Second, if religious zeal to persuade others of the
historical truth of the story results in omitting evidence
or misrepresenting it, the procedure is contrary to the
principles of research and scholarship.  This practice
lowers the standards in religion even farther!

Third, if we accept the Flood story as "true," then
we have a religion with a God who is a mass murderer!
It would be remarkable indeed if all people but one family
were so wicked that they deserved to be drowned.  Why
did God not reform mankind instead of destroying it ?  Or,
if mankind did deserve such punishment, why not send
a plague on it only, instead of killing with it nearly all
innocent animals, birds, and creeping things ?  We may
also ask, if the story were true, has the conduct of Noah's
descendants been much better than that of their prede-
cessors ?  Have the results justified the mass slaughter ?

Belief that God deliberately drowned nearly all of
mankind leads us to a serious theological problem.  One
of the reasons that God destroyed mankind, according to
Genesis 6:11 and 13, was because the earth was filled
with violence.  Yet God tried to solve the problem by being more violent than they--he drowned them all!  For a
god who condemned mankind for its violence and who for-
bade murder in the Ten Commandments, God set a very

bad example.  This problem of an unjust God was recognized early in Christianity, for at the close of the first century Clement of Rome tried to solve it.  He wrote: "Noah preached repentance, and as many as listened to him were saved" (1 Clement 7).  This places the responsibility on mankind; it had a chance to repent, but failed to do so.  This later rationalization is not in Genesis.

The effects of believing that the story is "true" are all negative.  They move religion in the direction of unintelligence and mediocrity.

When the story is told or read to children, they should be taught that the Flood is a story, not a historical event.  Adults should recognize that they have a responsibility to promote the development and future maturity of young minds.  Forcing children to believe that the story is "true" is unfair to them and hinders their intellectual growth.

Personally, I am glad that the world is not controlled by a God who once conducted a mass destruction of mankind.  But that is the kind of God we get from the belief that the Flood really happened.

The fundamentalist perspective of the Flood and other stories in the Bible attempts to make a Book of History out of a Book of Religion.

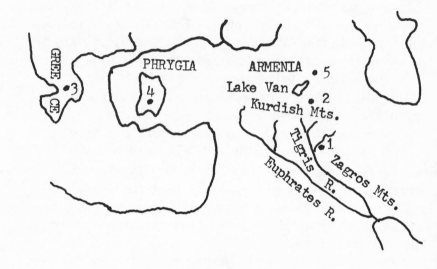

1. Mount Nisir
2. Mount Judi
3. Mount Parnassus
4. Apamea
5. Mount Ararat

FIGURE 1.   ALLEGED LANDING SITES

# CHAPTER 8

## THE MOUNTAIN MOVED TOO!

The Flood story is not the only element that traveled northward and westward. Within the story, the location of the mountain or mountains on which the boat landed moved too!

## ZAGROS MOUNTAINS

Whether the Sumerian version of the story mentioned that the boat landed on a mountain is uncertain, because in the fragment the description of the Flood breaks off just as Ziusudra is sacrificing bulls and sheep to the Sungod. If the sacrifice was performed on the boat, then a landing on a mountain or a mountain range may have followed in the lost portion. The location of the landing place would probably be the mountains east of Sumer. But if the sacrifice was performed on the ground, then the story did not mention a landing site.

In the earlier Babylonian version, Atrahasis, the description of the end of the Flood was in the missing section of Tablet III. Therefore we do not know whether a landing place was mentioned. In the later Babylonian version, which is in the Gilgamesh Epic, the ark lands on Mount Nisir, which was in the Zagros Mountains northeast of Babylonia. The mountain is no longer called Mount Nisir, and its precise location is unknown. Nevertheless, we do know from the annals of King Ashurnasirpal II of Assyria (883-859 B.C.) that he located it south of the Little Zab River. Alexander Heidel suggested that Mount Nisir is probably to be identified with Pir Omar Gudrun which has an altitude of about 9,000 feet.[48]

## ARMENIAN AND KURDISH MOUNTAINS: HARAN

As we know, the Hurrians migrated from Ararat
(Armenia; today in eastern Turkey) to northern Mesopotamia (today in northern Syria and northern Iraq).
They became acquainted with the Flood story and probably were the first to locate the landing in the mountains
of Ararat, their former homeland.  "The mountains of
Ararat" in the P source in Genesis is an expression that
is probably derived, either directly or indirectly, from
the Hurrian version.  As the story moved northward, the
location of the landing site moved northward too--a natural result of adaptation to local environment.   When the
Hebrews adopted the story, however, they did not change
the site to mountains in Palestine or Syria.  Thus the Hebrew tradition is an exception to the general pattern that
when the story moved, the landing site moved too.

In the third century B.C. Berossus, the Babylonian,
placed the landing in the Gordyaean (Kurdish) mountains
of Armenia, that is, the mountains of the Kurdish people
in Armenia.  In ancient times the Kurds did not live as
far north as they have wandered since, judging from ancient literary references to them, as James Bryce observed.[49]  They lived south of Lake Van, in the region
that is now southeastern Turkey and northern Iraq.  This
is a different region from that of Mount Ararat, which is
north of Lake Van.

We do not know who was the first to locate the landing in the mountains of the Kurds, but it must have been
people living in northern Mesopotamia, probably in the
first millenium B.C.  A plausible conjecture is that some
Assyrians were responsible; on the other hand, we know
that the Assyrians possessed the Babylonian version in
which the site was Mount Nisir, to the east.  These mountains were on the northern border of Mesopotamia and
were the highest that could be seen by people living on
the plain of northern Iraq, and thus were a natural choice.

The Jewish book, Jubilees, written in the latter half

of the second century B.C., states that the ark landed in
Ararat and gives the name of the mountain as "Lubar."
"And the ark went and rested on top of Lubar, one of the
mountains of Ararat" (Jub. 5:28). "Noah planted vines
on the mountain on which the ark had rested, named Lubar, one of the Ararat mountains, and they produced
fruit in the fourth year" (Jub. 7:1). The location of this
mountain is unknown. The Lubar tradition passed on to
the Christian writer, Epiphanius (Pan. 2. 1), and to the
Book of Noah in the Jewish Midrash. The same tradition
is in the Genesis Apocryphon (10. 12; 12. 13) in the Qumran scrolls. The author may have learned it from Jubilees, for Jubilees was one of the books in the library at
Qumran. The origin of this tradition is not clear. Perhaps the author of Jubilees (or a predecessor) tried to
update Genesis by selecting a particular mountain in Ararat, or perhaps he invented the name of the mountain,
or perhaps he combined the Genesis tradition with some
tradition about a Mount Lubar.

Josephus, the famous Jewish historian in the first
Christian century, knew and mentioned Berossus' ac-
count and the Flood story in the writings of Mnaseas,
Nicolaus of Damascus, and Hieronymous the Egyptian.
Josephus accepted Berossus' tradition that the ark land-
ed in the Kurdish mountains "in Armenia."[50]

Josephus reported that Nicolaus of Damascus wrote:

There is a great mountain in Armenia,
over Minyas, called Baris, upon which it
is reported that many who fled at the time
of the Deluge were saved; and that one who
was carried in an ark came on shore upon
the top of it; and that the remains of the
timber were a great while preserved. This
might be the man about whom Moses the
legislator of the Jews wrote.[51]

We do not know the location of the mountain "Baris."
In Cassuto's opinion, Mount Baris may perhaps be identified with the Mount Lubar listed in Jubilees; both names
contain the element bar. [52]

A continuation of the type of general tradition that
Berossus had transmitted, a reference to the Kurdish
mountains, occurs in two Jewish Targums, the Targum
of Onkelos and the Targum of Pseudo-Jonathan. These
Targums were second century A.D. Aramaic transla-
tions of the Pentateuch, written in Babylonia and Palestine, respectively. Both writings accept the tradition
that the ark landed on the mountains of the Kurds, as
does Genesis Rabbah (33.4) in the Jewish Midrash.

Sometimes what appear to the untrained eye as two
separate words are really two forms of the same word.
The matter is too complex to describe here, but two
important aspects should be mentioned. Hebrew and
Aramaic were consonantal languages, with three conso-
nants as the root, or basic form, of a word. Vowels
usually were not written, but their sound was supplied
when the word was vocalized, that is, spoken. When the
word was transliterated into the letters of another language, different writers might supply different vowels,
and sometimes writers differed in their choice of con-
sonants of similar sound. Also, more letters could be
attached to the beginning or end of a word. Thus Gordyaean, Cordene, Kadron, and Kurd are different tran-
scriptions of the same root, krd, and all mean Kurd"
or "Kurdish."

The Qur'an, or Koran, the sacred writings of the
Muslims, states that Noah's ark "settled on al-Judi"
(xi.46). The identity of the mountain referred to here
is not certain, but it is generally agreed that it was in
what is now northern Iraq or southeastern Turkey.
Nevertheless, tradition has selected a "Mount Judi." [53]
Cilo Dagi, in the southeastern corner of Turkey, may
be the "al-Judi" mentioned in the Qur'an. It is more
than 13,600 feet in height, the highest mountain on the

border between Armenia and Mesopotamia. To this day many Muslims and Syrian Christians believe that the ark landed on "Mount Judi." Is it identical with ancient "Mount Lubar" and/or "Mount Baris"?

Thus the notion that the ark settled on the mountains of the Kurds became a belief with a long and interesting history. It began outside of Judaism, before Christianity was born, among peoples living in northern Mesopotamia. It spread to the Jews after they became acquainted with it through the writings of various pagan writers. Jews passed it on to the Syrian Church, and it became the prevailing view in the Christian East. It has persevered into the modern world in the beliefs of the Nestorian Christians in northern Iraq. Finally, it was transmitted to the Muslims, who selected a specific mountain in the region as the site.

In one passage of his writings Josephus mentions remains of the ark at Carrhae, the Roman name for the ancient Hurrian city, Haran (modern name: Harran; in Turkey, near Syrian border). This suggests that there was a tradition that the boat landed at Haran. Was Armenia as the landing site an early Hurrian tradition, while Haran as the location was a later Hurrian tradition?

## MOUNT PARNASSUS

After the Flood story was transmitted to Greece, the Greeks relocated the landing site in their own region. In both Apollodorus' and Ovid's accounts the place is Mount Parnassus, a peak more than 8,000 feet in height. Mount Parnassus is located in central Greece, north of the Gulf of Corinth. The mountain was sacred to the Greek god Apollo Pythius. The famous Delphic oracle of Apollo was located on its slopes, as were also the Pythian games, which consisted of musical competitions as well as athletic and equestrian contests. Mount Parnassus is not quite so high as Mount Olympus, the home of the Greek gods, which is more than 9,500 feet high. Evidently Parnassus was selected because of its popularity as well as its height.

## APAMEA

A mountain near or in the city of Apamea in ancient Phrygia was another alleged landing site. The city was located in what is now west-central Turkey. As early as the time of Emperor Augustus it bore the cognomen Ki- botos, "Ark," which distinguished it from other cities named Apamea in Asia Minor and Syria.[54] Apamea ap- parently bore this label because its citizens claimed that the ark had landed there. As we saw at the close of chap- ter 5, this tradition continued at least into the third Chris- tian century. The Flood story was probably adapted to Apamea by its Jewish citizens, who either ignored or re- interpreted the expression "the mountains of Ararat" in Genesis, and proceeded to relocate the landing in Apamea. Writing around A.D. 220, the Christian author, Sextus Julius Africanus, mentioned that some people in his day said that the mountains of Ararat on which the ark land- ed are at Celaenae in Phrygia.[55] Celaenae was near Apamea.

## CHRISTIAN TRADITIONS

The earliest-known Christian references to the land- ing are confused as to the location. Theophilus, bishop of Antioch, who wrote around A.D. 180, placed it "in the Arabian mountains."[56] About fifty years later Sextus Julius Africanus, though he mentioned the Celaenae tra- dition, stated that "we know" the mountains of Ararat on which the ark landed are "in Parthia"[57] (Parthia was in the region of modern Iran). The apparent cause of the confusion is that these writers, following Genesis, believed that the site was "the mountains of Ararat," but they did not know where Ararat was. In Roman times that country was generally called "Armenia," not "Ararat."

When Christianity came to Armenia, it introduced the inhabitants to the Bible. The Armenians connected the "Ararat" of Genesis with their own district, but they made free use of the term by applying it to a particular mountain. Christians seem to have been the first to locate the landing on "Mount Ararat" in northern Armenia, northeast of Lake Van. By the fourth century, the Christian tradition existed that the ark had come to rest there. Nevertheless, the tradition was not universally adopted then by Christians, for Epiphanius still gave only the general location for the site, "the country of the Kurds." Mount Ararat is close to the juncture of the borders of three modern countries: Turkey, the Soviet Union, and Iran. Its Armenian name is Mount Massis, and its Turkish name is Agri-dagh, or Agri Dagi. Its highest peak has an altitude of about 16,900 feet.

It is not difficult to detect the reason for changing the site from the Armenian mountains or the Kurdish mountains in general to Agri-dagh in northeastern Armenia. The reason, as Heidel recognized, [58] is the mountain's height. What would seem more logical to believers than the idea that the ark must have landed on the highest mountain in the area and that the peak should be called "Mount Ararat"? The fact that the Romans no longer called the region Ararat probably facilitated the transfer of the name to a particular mountain.

Traditionalists are certain to be surprised and shocked to learn that Mount Ararat is the last--not the first--of the various main sites that have been chosen as the landing place of the boat that carried the survivors of the Flood to safety. The basis for selecting Agri-dagh was not memory, or oral or written transmission of an original tradition, but a deduction from the mountain's

height, a deduction made more than two millenia after
the story began.

Thus the landing site moved from Iraq to Armenia in
general, to the Kurdish mountains, to Syria, to Greece,
to Apamea, and finally to northeastern Armenia. Within
the process of transferring the sites, an important psychological trait was at work. The tendency to change
tradition from the general to the particular was a common trait in the ancient world. When stories were transmitted either orally or in writing, details were added
that were not in the original, and sometimes general
statements were transformed into direct quotations. When
scribes copied manuscripts, they inserted specific features such as names of persons, even though they often
had no basis in fact for doing so. Similarly, in respect
to the landing place of the ark, the general tended to become particular. The mountains of the Kurds became a
specific peak, Mount Judi, within those mountains. The
"mountains of Ararat" in Genesis became a specific
mountain within Ararat. Even scholars have often missed
the distinction between the general reference to the Kurdish mountains and the specific reference to Mount Judi.
Needless to say, Christians through the centuries have
ignored the distinction between the general "mountains
of Ararat" in the Bible, and the specific place, "Mount
Ararat," of later tradition.

If the Flood had actually occurred, the only probable
mountain on which to find the boat or ark would be the one
on which it had landed. If the location was recorded, it
would be found in the earliest, or at least one of the earliest, of the accounts. And the earliest-known identifica-
tion of the landing site is Mount Nisir, in modern Iraq.

But the tradition that the ark landed far to the north,
on Mount Ararat in modern Turkey, is the latest of the
traditional sites. This fact in itself should tell us something about the probability--or rather, the improbability--
of finding the remains of the ark on "Mount Ararat."

# CHAPTER 9

## MOUNT ARARAT

Before looking at the history of the efforts to find the remains of Noah's ark, we need some knowledge of the nature of Mount Ararat. Although this mountain is not the first one for which claims were made, it apparently is the only one on which much search for the ark has been conducted. Information about the general characteristics of the mountain will be useful as background for understanding the search efforts.

Actually there are two mountains called "Ararat," which are side by side: Little Ararat and Great Ararat. The name "Mount Ararat" is ususally applied only to Great Ararat, because it is much higher than the other. These two peaks are about seven miles apart. Little Ararat is about 12,900 feet and Great Ararat about 16,900 feet in height. The saddle where the two mountains join varies from about 7,000 to 8,000 feet in altitude. Together the two mountains form a land mass about twenty-five miles in length and about twelve miles in width, in a line running from northwest to southeast. They are surrounded by the Aras plain.

The two mountains were formed by volcanic action within the last two million years. From the standpoint of geologic time, the formation is comparatively recent, for the earth is hundreds of millions of years old. After these mountains were formed, additional volcanic activity occurred. Cones of small volcanoes remain between the two peaks. Movement of rock caused by geologic pressure, together with continuing eruptions, transformed Great Ararat, in James Bryce's words, from a symmetrical cone into "a huge, broad-shouldered mass, more of a dome than a cone, supported by strong buttresses, and throwing out rough ribs or ridges of rock that stand out like

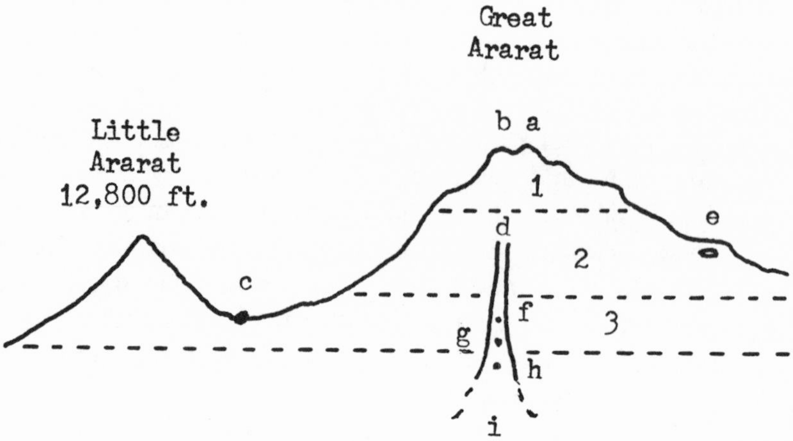

Zone 1. Glaciers and snow, 14,000 feet to top
Zone 2. Boulders, 10,000 to 14,000 feet
Zone 3. Grazing, 6,000 to 10,000 feet

a. West summit, 16,900 feet
b. East summit, 40 feet below the west summit
c. Sardar Bulakh, a camp, 7,500 feet
d. Ahora Gorge
e. Lake Kop
f. Jacob's Well
g. Ahora (village site)
h. St. James Monastery, ruins of
i. Ahora Valley

FIGURE 2.    MOUNT ARARAT

knotty muscles from its solid trunk."59

Later a tremendous new eruption occurred on Great
Ararat; it came out not at the summit, but out of a long
chasm that opened on the northeast side. A tremendous
amount of rock and ash were blasted out, leaving the deep
gulch known as the Ahora, or Ahore, Gorge, several miles
in length, running longitudinally down the mountain. When
the snow melts in the spring and summer, a stream flows
down the gorge and into the Aras River.

Warm air from the plain, heated by the sun, rushes
up the sides of Great Ararat. When it reaches the snow
and ice, the air condenses and forms clouds, which hov-
er on the mountain top from a few hours after sunrise until sunset. The clouds disappear at night, and the white
peak contrasts beautifully with the dark blue sky.


## THE THREE ZONES

The surface of Great Ararat is divided into three
zones. The first zone, the peak, is perpetually covered
with ice and snow. The glaciers in it are several hundred feet thick. This zone extends from about 14,000
feet up to the west summit, 16,946 feet above sea level.

The second zone, the middle of the mountain, ranges
in altitude from about 10,000 to 14,000 feet. Boulders
cover it throughout. It has some snow in winter, but in
summer it is bare and dry. The melting snow produces
numerous small brooks which could water the mountainside if the surface permitted them to do so. The volcanic rock, however, is so porous that the brooks quickly
disappear into the mountain. Consequently this zone is
very dry, without vegetation. Lake Kop, or Lake Kip,
which is really only a pool, is in this zone on the northwest side of the mountain. Its altitude is about 12,200
feet. Around and below Lake Kop is a plateau, Kip Göl.

The third zone is a grazing area, ranging from the
base of the mountain (6,000 feet or less) to about 10,000

feet above sea level. Here the Kurds graze their flocks
of sheep and goats, moving them progressively up the
mountain during the dry season. A military camp, Sardar Bulakh, is in this zone, at an altitude of about 7,500
feet in the saddle between Little Ararat and Great Ararat.
A good spring is located there, which is a major reason
that Cossacks and Kurds have camped at the place through
the years. The camp is surrounded by a plain with good
grass for pasture. The name, Sardar Bulakh, is Persian
in origin and means "Governor's Well" or "Governor's
Spring." James Bryce suggested that the site probably
acquired its name when some Persian governor long ago
stationed a garrison there. [60] In the nineteenth century
when Russia controlled this part of the mountain, this
spot was a Cossack military camp; today it is a Turkish
post. When Abich (1845) and Bryce (1876) climbed Great
Ararat, they used this camp as their base of operations.
Kurdish shepherds also have camps in the grazing zone.

In this same zone the Ahora Gorge opens up to form
the Ahora Valley. Jacob's Well, which is really a spring,
is at the head of the valley at an altitude of about 7,500
feet. Below it there was once a village called Arghuri,
or Ahuri, with about two hundred houses. Still lower in
the Ahora Valley are the remains of St. James' Monastery, which belonged to the Armenian Christians. When
Friedrich Parrot made the first modern ascension of
Great Ararat, in 1829, the monastery was still standing,
and he used it as his headquarters.

On June 20, 1840, a strong earthquake, followed by
a blast of wind and the falling of masses of rock loosed
suddenly from the Ahora Gorge, destroyed both the village and the monastery. No one survived. Snow and ice
which were precipitated to the lower slopes melted in a
few days, forming torrents of water and mud which flowed
out into the Aras plain. The earthquake and flood together
leveled the buildings and covered them with mud and rock.
The village and monastery remain desolate in their ruins.

## DIFFICULTY OF CLIMBING MOUNT ARARAT

Of the two Ararats, Great Ararat is the one men usually seek to climb.  Nevertheless, several factors make
ascension of the mountain very difficult.  Its altitude is
more than three miles.  At such heights breathing is difficult and muscular effort strenuous.  Violent storms fre-
quently arise suddenly on the mountain, especially on the
south slope and the summit.  Some of the terrain is steep
and rugged; in some places loose rocks impede progress.
In some areas steps must be cut in the ice with ice axes
in order to ascend; with that procedure advance is inev-
itably slow.  Climbers usually try to reach a good height
on one day, then sleep on the cold mountainside.  The
next day they begin the final assault as early as possible
in order to reach the summit (hopefully before an early
afternoon storm arrives) and descend to a camp by night-
fall, glissading, or sliding, part of the way.  Even the
middle zone offers problems: poisonous snakes thrive
among the rocks.  Montgomery reports that when he ascended Mount Ararat in 1970, a poisonous snake killed
one of the pack mules. [61]

The tradition was established early among the Armenian Christians that no one can climb Mount Ararat.  In
the fourth century Faustus of Byzantium told the story of
St. Jacob, the bishop of Nisibis, who tried in vain to
ascend the mountain to see Noah's ark.  Jacob's Well and
the Monastery of St. James (i.e., St. Jacob; "James"
is an English transcription of the ancient name Jacob)
are named in his honor.  According to the story, an angel
told him when he was on the mountainside, that it was the
will of the Lord that he should cease wanting to see the
ark.  Jacob returned down the mountain, without reaching the summit.  Thus in the fourth century Armenians
believed that it was impossible to ascend to the summit
and that it was against God's will to try.

In the Middle Ages the tradition took two forms.  One
view was that Jacob--and only Jacob--had succeeded in
climbing Mount Ararat.  Vincent of Beauvais in the thirteenth century and Sir John Mandeville in the fourteenth
held that opinion.  The majority of the writers in the Middle Ages who mention the subject, however, took the view
that no one had ascended to the top.  If they gave a reason
for this fact, the reason is the nature of the mountain,
especially the snow and ice on its peak and the precipices
on its sides.  Any commandment from God against the
effort was generally not mentioned.

Both forms of the Armenian tradition continued into
the nineteenth cnetury.  James Bryce in 1877 remarked
that "it has long been almost an article of faith with the
Armenian Church that the top of Ararat is inaccessible."[62]
He reported that a few days after he ascended Great Ararat, he visited the Armenian monastery of Echmiadzin
nearby.  When the head of the monastery was told that
Bryce had just climbed to the top, the old monk replied,
"No, that cannot be.  No one has ever been there.  It is
impossible."[63]

# CHAPTER 10

## FIND THAT ARK!

The notion that the ark, or remnants of it, survived through the centuries is not a new idea. There is no evidence that the Sumerians or the early Babylonians made such a claim, however; this is understandable, for they regarded the Flood as a story or poem. Later, after the Flood was viewed as a historical event, the claim that the ark continued to exist seemed to be proof that such an event occurred. The incorporation of the story in Hebrew writings that were eventually canonized as Scripture undoubtedly fostered belief in the Flood as history. Local pride was further cause of the claim that remains could still be seen; the unsupported claim could be made that the ark was somewhere on some mountains or was on top of a mountain too high to climb, and relics could be displayed as alleged remnants of the ark. By the third century B. C. , at least, the claim was well established, for Berossus transmitted the tradition that some of the boat still remained in the Kurdish mountains of Armenia. He stated, too, that people were scraping pitch from it and were making amulets from the pitch. In the next few centuries other pagan writers passed on the belief without question.

In the first century A. D. the Jewish writer, Josephus, quoted the tradition from Berossus and accepted it, but he reinterpreted it as a reference to Noah's ark. He added that "a great many" writers mention the same thing. Then he proceeded to quote Nicolaus of Damascus, who, as we have seen, wrote that remains of the wood of the ark were preserved for "a great while. "[64] Nicolaus' statement implies that the remains no longer existed in his day. In another passage in his writing Josephus wrote that in the district called Carron [evidently a form

of the name Carrhae] the remains of Noah's ark were
still being shown to those who desired to see them. [65]
Carrhae was a town in northern Mesopotamia, southwest of Armenia; thus Carrhae was an additional place
where remnants of the ark were claimed to exist. Some
writers have tried to change Josephus' spelling to make
it fit "Gordyaene" or "Cordyene," so that it would locate
the mountain in Armenia. Such radical change in the
spelling appears to be unjustified.

## EARLY CHRISTIAN TRADITIONS

Late in the second century A.D. Theophilus of Antioch wrote that the remains of the ark "are to this day to
be seen in the Arabian mountains."[66] As we observed in
chapter 8, the word "Arabian" here is probably a misunderstanding of the term "Ararat." Considering that he
did not even know what country the ark was supposed to be
in, we may safely conclude that Theophilus had not seen
any of its remains.

Early in the third century Hippolytus in Rome wrote:
"Both the dimensions and relics of this ark, as we have
explained, are shown to this day in the mountains called
Ararat, which are situated in the direction of the country
of the Adiabeni."[67] The Adiabeni lived in Adiabene, the
district between the two Zab Rivers, near the north end
of the Zagros Mountains. Adiabene is of interest to us
here because it was closer to the Babylonian landing site,
Mount Nisir, than it was to what became the Christian
landing site, Mount Ararat.

In the latter half of the fourth century two more Christian writers claimed that remains of the ark still existed.
Chrysostom located them in the mountains of Armenia, [68]
and Epiphanius stated that remnants were still being
shown in "the country of the Kurds."[69]

With the passage of time, Christian beliefs generally reached agreement on Mount Ararat as the site, fol-

lowing the lead of the Armenian Christians. The claim
continued to be made that remains of the ark were on the
mountain top and that they were being shown. The claim
fostered conservative religious faith, but it also created
a problem. After a specific mountain was selected as the
site, some of the faithful wanted to climb it and see the
ark. As we have seen, Mount Ararat is very difficult to
climb. Considering the lack of adequate equipment in ancient times, the probablility is slight that anyone actually
ascended to the summit. Nevertheless, some may have
tried and were disappointed when they failed to see the ark
from a distance.

A solution was to discourage people from trying to
climb the mountain. An example is found in a fragment
(ascribed to Hippolytus, but probably not written by him)
of a commentary on the Pentateuch. It contains a statement that is interesting as an early admission that, although devotees still believed that remains of the ark
were on the mountain, the belief could not be verified.
The author warned the readers that if anyone tries to ascend, demons will throw him down the mountain and kill
him.

> As to Mount Kardu, it is in the east, in the
> land of the sons of Raban, and the Orientals
> call it Mount Godash; the Arabians and Per-
> sians call it Ararat. And there is a town of
> the name Kardu, and that hill is called after
> it, which is indeed very lofty and inaccessible,
> whose summit no one has ever been able to
> reach, on account of the violence of the winds
> and the storms which always prevail there.
> And if anyone attempts to ascend it, there are
> demons that rush upon him, and cast him
> down headlong from the ridge of the mountain
> into the plain, so that he dies. No one,
> moreover, knows what there is on the top of
> the mountain, except that certain relics of the

wood of the ark still lie there on the surface of the top of the mountain.[70]

If no one had climbed the mountain and no one knew what
was up there, how could anyone be so sure that relics of
the wood of the ark were at the top?

Early in the fourth century Saint Jacob, bishop of
Nisibis, was very eager to find the ark on Mount Ararat.
The story of his attempt to climb the mountain was told
later in the fourth century by Faustus of Byzantium. According to the story, Jacob and his companions became
very tired and thirsty as they were ascending. He knelt
and prayed to God. At the spot where his head touched
the ground, a spring of water burst forth. Consequently,
according to Faustus, the spring in his day was called
[as it is today] "Jacob's Well." As he ascended, Jacob
prayed continually, asking God to let him see the ark.
When he was near the summit, he became exhausted and
fell asleep. An angel appeared and told him that the Lord
had heard his prayer and was bringing to pass what he desired. The angel said that he had brought Jacob a piece
of wood from the ark, and that Jacob would find it on his
pallet. [This was hardly equivalent to seeing the whole
ark.] The angel gave him a commandment from God: he
must stop wanting to see the ark. Jacob and his companions took the piece of wood down the mountain and gave
it to the joyful crowd from the nearby city and countryside
who came out to meet him. Looking upon him as a great
prophet who had seen God, they embraced him and kissed
his feet. The crowd was delighted to receive this gift of
the holy wood. Faustus stated that the people still preserved this piece of wood in his day as a remnant of the
ark of Noah.[71]

The story has a different device for discouraging attempts to find the ark on Mount Ararat. Instead of in-
stilling fear of demons up there, it describes the Lord
himself as commanding even a saint to stop wanting to
see the ark. Thus, by forbidding people to climb and in-

vestigate, faith in the ark's continued existence was pro-
tected. No one could disprove the belief. Another motive for discouraging efforts to ascend the mountain, however, probably was the hazardous nature of the mountain,
as Balsiger and Sellier suggest. [72] The physical injuries
and loss of life resulting from attempts to reach the summit, would lead to a desire to save others from similar
misfortunes.

The legend of Saint Jacob of Nisibis is significant in
another respect. The story represents early use of relics as a solution to the problem of not finding the ark.
The explanation, in effect, is: "I cannot show you the ark,
but here is a piece of the wood." This device has been
popular through the centuries.

## FROM THE 7TH TO 17TH CENTURIES

Through the Middle Ages a few writers continued to
claim that remains of the ark could still be seen on Mount
Ararat. The claim was made by Isidore of Seville, a
Christian encyclopedist in the seventh century. In the
thirteenth century both the encyclopedist Vincent of Beauvais and the Franciscan monk William of Rubruck briefly transmitted the legend of Saint Jacob. Vincent's form
of it is garbled, however. According to Vincent, the
monk succeeded in finding the ark; after Jacob returned
from ascending the mountain, he built a monastery as a
holy relic. Another thirteenth-century monk, Jehan
Haithon, wrote that no one could climb Mount Ararat,
but a large black object, which was reported to be Noah's
ark, could be seen at the top. [72a] Similarly, in the four-

teenth-century composite work ascribed to Sir John Mandeville, a writer remarks that the ark could be seen on
the mountain from "afar in clear weather." He was
skeptical, though, of claims that men had touched the
ark: " . . . some men say that they have seen and
touched the ship, and put their fingers in the parts where

the fiend went out, when that Noah said <u>Benedicte</u>. But they that say such words, say their will." The writer added that no one since Noah has gone up the mountain, except one monk [Jacob], and therefore "men should not believe such words."[73]

In the seventeenth century Adam Olearius, a German scholar, wrote an account of his travels and observations while serving as an ambassador to Muscovy and to Persia. He reported that the Armenians and Persians believed that there were still remainders of the ark on Ararat, but that time had so hardened them that they seemed "absolutely petrify'd." He remarked that at Schamachy in Persia he was shown a cross made of black, hard wood, "which the Inhabitants affirmed to have been made of the Wood of the Ark: and upon that account it was look'd upon as a most precious Relick, and, as such, was wrapped in Crimson Taffata [taffeta]. The Mountain is now inaccessible, by reason of the precipices whereby it is encompass'd of all sides."[74]

In the seventeenth century Christian monks were coming from various countries to live as hermits on the sacred mountain, Mount Ararat. The Dutch traveler, Jan Janszoon Struys, had an interesting encounter with one of them. Domingo Alessandro, a monk from Rome, had lived on the mountain for twenty-five years, and unfortunately, had just developed a hernia. About the same time, Struys was having troubles of his own. While traveling in the Middle East he was taken prisoner and sold as a slave to a Persian. His master tried in vain to sell him in Ervan, or Erivan, a town near Mount Ararat. There two Carmelite monks asked if he was a surgeon, and he said he was not. Nevertheless, they offered his master a cash present of fifty crowns if his slave would heal a friend of his hernia. The master then promised Struys his freedom if he effected a cure. "Trusting in the good grace of God, and hoping for a lucky success," Struys "consented to take the Patient in hand." The trip up to Alessandro's cave took seven days. Each night

the party stayed in the hut of a hermit farther up the mountain.  Each morning a hermit would supply them with a
different peasant as a guide for the day and a fresh donkey
to carry their provisions and wood.  When they reached
Alessandro, Struys hard-boiled two hundred fresh hens'
eggs [ ?] and made a truss.  Four times a day he anoint-
ed the hermit with an unguent made from the eggs, and
he made him lie still for a fortnight.  Then the hermit
felt better and Struys ordered him to wear the truss for a
whole year and to continue anointing himself.  The hermit
rewarded him with the only gift he could give: a dark red,
wooden cross suspended from a silver chain he wore
around his neck, a cross the monk said that he himself
had made from "a piece of the wood of the true Ark of
Noah." He wrote a statement for Struys, saying that "I
myself entered that Ark and with my own hands cut from
the wood of one of its compartments the fragment from
which that cross is made." He also gave Struys a piece
of the rock from under the ark.  The monk also suggested that if Struys would take these relics to Saint Peter's
Church at Rome, he would receive handsome compensa-
tion. [75]

Struys reported an Armenian modernization of an old
tradition.  Whereas in Berossus' tradition people were
making amulets from the pitch of the ark, in the seventeenth century the Armenians were saying that people made
a powder from the pitch and were taking it to preserve
their health.  Thus in the later age when people were beginning to rely more on medicine than charms, the tradition was changed accordingly.

None of the Christian writers in this period climbed
the mountain (although Struys went up part way to see a
hermit) or claimed to have personally seen the ark.  They
merely repeated traditions transmitted from the distant
past.  At least two writers were shown relics alleged to

have been made from the ark.

Some Muslim writers during the tenth to thirteenth
centuries were less extravagant in their assertions.
Their typical claim on the subject was that one could see
"the place" on the mountain where the ark had landed. [76]
Rabbi Benjamin of Tudela (12th c.), however, reported a
wild Muslim story about an Omar Ben al-Khatab who took
the ark from the top of two mountains [the mountains of
two different traditions ?] and built a mosque of it. [77]

## NINETEENTH CENTURY

In the nineteenth century a new phase began: men succeeded in reaching the summit of Mount Ararat. Some
were looking for the ark, and others simply wanted to
climb the mountain.

The first person to ascend to the top in modern
times--and probably the first ever--was J. J. Friedrich
Parrot, in 1829. He was Professor of Natural Philoso-
phy at the University of Dorpat (modern name of the city:
Tartu) in the Estonian region of Russia. He climbed up
the northwest side of Great Ararat and reached its highest peak. He kept a detailed record of the expedition,
and afterwards described the ascent in his book, Journey
to Ararat. He was an orthodox believer in the historicity
of the Flood and the existence of Noah's ark on Mount Ararat. When he failed to find the ark, he concluded that it
might still be under the glaciers on the peak. He mani-
fested his piety by erecting a wooden cross on the summit
and by holding a prayer meeting with his party there.

Seven years later the East India Company's Resident
at Bagdad, Claudius James Rich, lived and traveled in
the Middle East for many years, and he reported that
his Muslim guide in Kurdistan claimed that he had seen
the remains of Noah's ark. The mountain mentioned may
be Mount Judi; it certainly is not Mount Ararat, which
could not possibly be ascended in "an hour." Rich de-

scribed the report in his notebook as follows:

> Hussein Aga maintained to me that he has
> with his own eyes seen the remains of Noah's
> Ark.  He went to a Christian village, whence
> he ascended by a steep road of an hour to the
> summit, on which he saw the remains of a
> very large vessel of wood almost entirely
> rotted, with nails a foot long still remain-
> ing. [78]

In 1845 O. W. H. Abich, a geologist at the University
of Dorpat, started from camp Sardar Bulakh and climbed
up the southeastern slope of Great Ararat.  He was the
first to reach its eastern peak, which therefore has been
named for him.  His interest was scientific.  The difficulty of climbing the mountain is indicated by the fact
that Parrot had to try three times and Abich four times
in order to make the ascent.  Abich erected a seven-foot
cross near the peak, but saw no ark.

In 1850 Colonel Khodzko, with sixty Russian soldiers, conducted a successful expedition up the mountain.
This group, too, carried a cross up the mountain and
erected it at the top.  An English party of five, led by
Major Robert Stuart, ascended six years later.  Both expeditions followed Abich's route up, except Major Frazer
in the English party.  Neither expedition found any ark,
but Stuart's party saw the oak cross erected by Abich.

In 1876 James Bryce, the famous author and professor of law at Oxford University, climbed Great Ararat.
At an altitude of more than 13,000 feet he found a stick
four feet long and five inches thick; he gleefully thought
it probably was from the ark.  He suggested the theory
that if there were any remains of the ark on the mountain,
they probably would be down on the slopes instead of at
the summit, carried down by the movement of snow and
ice.  He admitted that another possible cause could account for the stick, but declined to give it:

> I am, however, bound to admit that an-
> other explanation of the presence of this
> piece of timber on the rocks at this vast
> height did occur to me. But as no man
> is bound to discredit his own relic [sic],
> and such is certainly not the practice of
> the Armenian Church, I will not disturb
> my readers' minds, or yield to the ra-
> tionalizing tendencies of the age by sug-
> gesting it.[79]

In 1888 E. de Markoff, a Russian geographer, climb
ed the mountain and saw no ark. He did find a stick, how
ever. He found the stick on which two previous Russian ex
plorers had carved their initials; he concluded that originally it probably was from the cross Abich had planted.

In 1893 Henry Lynch, a British merchant engaged in
trade with the Middle East, also ascended Great Ararat.
He found a metal plate, inscribed in Russian, affixed to
the rocks by Markoff's expedition. As he stood on the sum
mit, Lynch was confident that he was on the spot where the
ark landed--but he found no evidence of it.

John Joseph Nouri, an archdeacon in the Nestorian
church in Malabar, India, claimed that after three unsuc-
cessful attempts, he had climbed Mount Ararat. He reportedly stood in awe as he gazed on the ark lodged in the
rocks, half filled with ice and snow. He went inside and
took careful measurements, which coincided exactly with
those given in the biblical story of Noah. [80] He gave lec-
tures on his "marvelous discovery" in the chapel of the
Presbyterian College at Lake Urmia in Persia. Next he
tried to organize a company in Belgium that would get the
ark and transport it to the World's Columbian Exposition
in Chicago in 1893. Fortunately, the Belgians had better
judgment than to waste their money on such a foolish project. This was fortunate for Nouri too, saving him the
embarrassment of leading an expedition to the mountain
and finding no ark.

## TWENTIETH CENTURY

Some explorers and scientists climbed Great Ararat in this century too, beginning with the Russian scientist, Ivangouloff, in 1902, who placed recording thermometers on its summit. Louis Seylaz ascended in 1910. Oliver S. Crosby in 1951 climbed to within 150 feet of the summit. In 1966 the Oxford University Exploration Club organized an expedition to search for Christopher Trease, who had disappeared in August 1965 while attempting to climb Mount Ararat alone without proper equipment. This group went up the southwest side as far as the snowline. An eager believer who explored Mount Ararat tenaciously was John Libi. He thought that the exact location of the ark was divinely revealed to him in a dream. He searched in vain repeatedly, and made his seventh and final climb in 1969, at the age of 73. [81] John Warwick Montgomery climbed Ararat in 1970 and explored it in 1971. No one on these ascents observed any remains of an ark.

Nevertheless, some others--usually ark believers-- claimed that they had seen the ark or remnants of it on Great Ararat.

During World War II a story was printed in some papers stating that in World War I, in 1916, a Russian airman named Vladimir Roskovitsky had sighted the remains of the ark on a slope when he flew over Mount Ararat. According to the story, the Czar organized an expedition which climbed up and found the ark in 1917. The expedition's report, however, could not be found, and the claim was made that the report was lost in the Russian Revolution of 1917. André Parrot, a very reliable archaeologist and competent scholar, rejected the story as untrue, and commented:

All we have is Roskovitsky's story, of which

the least that can be said is that if it is shorn
of reminiscences of Genesis, scarcely anything is left.  That did not prevent several
American periodicals from proclaiming
the sensational news.  Serious specialist
organs reserved for it the fate it deserved:
silence. [82]

Thus André Parrot deduced that the Bible, not Roskovitsky's personal observation of something on Mount Ararat,
was the source of his description of the ark.  Wide circulation was given the news about the airman's claim and an
official Russian expedition.  According to Professor John
Bright, the report was published in Defender of the Faith
(Oct. 1942), The King's Herald (Nov. 1941), and Prophec
(Mar. 1942), but later two of these magazines retracted
the story.  Bright remarked:

The story is quite without foundation and, in-
asmuch as at least two of the above publications have printed retractions of it, it de-
serves no further notice.  It may be regarded
as a symptom of man's willingness to believe
what he wishes to believe. [83]

Commenting on the report in the above magazines, Pa
rot adds:

These periodicals had in fact been preceded
by the Kölnische Illustrierte Zeitung, which
had, on 1 April 1933, announced the discovery of Noah's Ark on Mount Ararat.  However, I have it from Pastor C. Berron (Bas-
Rhin), that this was an April Fool's Day
joke. [84]

Montgomery relates that he investigated a report in
in the Chicago Tribune (Mar. 29, 1953) and found it to be

erroneous.  The report stated that documentation concerning the Russian expedition to Ararat had been given
to the library of the University of Geneva by General Os-
nobichine, an aide to the Grand Duke Cyril.  A year's
research by Montgomery disproved the claim. [85]

Montgomery also cites correspondence from the files
of Eryl and Violet Cummings pertaining to the alleged
Russian expedition.  The Cummings have for many years
collected material pertaining to sightings of the ark on
Ararat, according to Montgomery and others.  In the letters cited, several persons testify that they had known
either John Schilleroff or a John Georgesen (both de-
ceased),  who told them that he was in a party of Russian
soldiers who saw the ark on Ararat.  Statements from a
former Russian army officer, Alexander Koor, are also
quoted from the Cummings' file. [86]

There are important discrepancies in that material.
In Koor's document the Russian aviator who first sighted
the ark is not Roskovitsky, but a First Lieutenant Zabo-
lotsky.  According to the letters, there were two, not one,
military expeditions to the mountain to look for the ark.
(The reason for this change in the tradition is apparent.
The logic is that Schilleroff and Georgesen belonged to
different expeditions, their stories agree, and therefore
the story is confirmed by two sources, not just one!)
One letter states that the ark was in a wooded valley
swamp high on the mountain; the storyteller must not
have ever seen the mountain, because there is no wooded valley high on barren Mount Ararat!  The reports
disagree on the location of the ark: high on the mountain
vs. the saddle between the two mountains.  When this
Cummings material is compared with an interview with
Roskovitsky published in Balsiger and Sellier's book, [87]
still more discrepancies appear: the ark was in a dense
swamp vs. it was in the overflow of a lake; the men
could not get to it because of the water, poisonous snakes,
and insects vs. they took complete measurements of the
ark and explored its rooms (from poultry size to ten

times elephant size).  One also wonders why people waited more than twenty years to make such great news
known.  All that this material seems to demonstrate is
that some people were great storytellers.

In 1932 the American traveler, Carveth Wells, visited the Armenian monastery at Echmiadzin near Ararat
to see the relic of the ark that Friedrich Parrot had reported was shown to him when he climbed the mountain in
1829.  The monastery had shown Parrot a small rectangular piece of wood hanging between the thumb and fore-
finger of Saint Jacob.  The wood was claimed to be the
very wood that the angel had given to Saint Jacob, which
Jacob brought with him when he descended the mountain.
When Wells visited the monastery a century later, Archbishop Mesrop showed him a piece of petrified wood about
twelve inches by nine inches, one inch thick, carefully
preserved in a golden reliquary.  Archbishop Mesrop
said that this relic was  "the portion of Noah's ark which
was brought down from Ararat by one of our monks named
Jacob, St. Jacob" (but it did not fit the description of the
piece shown to Parrot).  The archbishop said that he had
climbed Mount Ararat in 1913.  When asked if he had seen
the ark, he replied, "Too much snow and ice.  If there
are any remains, they must be buried under it. "[88]

Montgomery presents an account, based on the Cummings files, about a New Zealander, Hardwicke Knight,
who was exploring Mount Ararat in the late 1930s.  Knight
reported that in an ice field near Lake Kop he found em-
bedded in the ice some soggy timbers forming a rectangular frame like that of a very heavy wagon.  He broke
off a piece of the wood, but somehow this evidence has
not survived.  Later he became convinced that it was from
Noah's ark, and that a larger section of the ark might be
higher up the mountain under the ice.

Balsiger and Sellier report that an [unnamed] aviator in the Russian Air Force had shown photographs taken
from the air in 1938 and in 1947 or 1948; these photos
purportedly showed the ark protruding from a glacier.

In one photo, according to the report, the ark had holes
in the side and in the top. The aviator would not allow
copies to be made because, he said, the photographs
were the property of the USSR.[89]

As we might expect, reports arose that aviators in
World War II sighted the ark. Keller mentions reports
from a Russian pilot and four American fliers.[90] Also,
as we might expect, concrete evidence is mysteriously
missing! No first-hand descriptions exist; no photographs of it exist. Balsiger and Sellier mention a report that a sighting of the ark was described in a summer edition of Stars and Stripes, the U.S. Army newspaper. At the request of those authors, Mrs. Roberta
Shearin searched for the article in at least four editions;
she found no such report.[91]

The same authors report that a Kurdish farmer told
villagers that in September 1948 he saw the prow of a
ship extending from a canyon in the mountain. Then the
villagers climbed up, looked, and returned to proclaim
that it was a ship indeed. But, of course, none of the
villagers had a camera and took a picture.[92] (And they
must not have told anyone who had a camera either!)

Dr. Aaron Smith, a retired missionary from North
Carolina, thought that he had a divine revelation which
ordered him to go and search for the remains of the ark.
He organized an expedition which explored Mount Ararat
in the summer of 1949. André Parrot pointed out that
the mission was a complete failure, which French newspapers reported under headlines such as "Explorers
give up search for Noah's Ark," "No Ark in sight," and
"Noah's Ark not at rendezvous." Le Monde (September
24, 1949) stated that "the funds necessary for such an
expedition were easily found, since certain enthusiasts
had no hesitation in selling their peaceful businesses in
order to join the explorers."[93] Like Cummings, he extensively collected materials on Noah's ark. In 1951,
with 40 companions, he spent 12 days on the ice cap of
Great Ararat.[93a]

In the same year the faith in the existence of the ark on Ararat was dealt another blow, but from a different direction. Two Turkish journalists claimed that they saw the ark, but it was on Mount Judi. The report was in the Paris newspaper, <u>France-Soir</u> (August 31, 1949), under the headline: WE HAVE SEEN NOAH'S ARK . . . BUT NOT ON MOUNT ARARAT. The journalists said that they saw a vessel 500 feet long, 80 feet wide, and 50 feet high, and that they were shown Noah's tomb a few miles away. [94]

Montgomery reports from the Cummings files the case of George Jefferson Greene, an American mining engineer. While reconnoitering in a heliocopter in 1952, he saw on a ledge in the side of a cliff an object protruding from a glacier. Flying close to it, he took photographs from different angles, for he thought that it was the prow of Noah's ark. When the pictures were enlarged, the object was rectangular in shape with laminated sides. After failing to persuade friends to form an expedition to go with him to examine the "ark" more closely, he went to British Guiana, where he was murdered. The news of the "discovery" was not made public, however, and the photographs disappeared. Later Fred Drake, who said that he had seen the photos, sketched from memory for Mr. Cummings a side view and an end view of the object on the ledge, showing lamination or planking. [95]

In 1952 the French industrialist and amateur explorer, Fernand Navarra, ascended Great Ararat. At an altitude of about 13,800 feet he saw a huge black patch in the ice. He was convinced that he had found the ark, for the shape of the patch was that of a ship's hull, with curved sides [but the ark's sides would be straight, according to the Genesis description of it as a rectangular box]. Nevertheless, some good came from this trip, for Navarra disproved a claim that the monks at the monastery of Echmiadzin had been making. They had used their telescope to show visitors a black object on the

western face of the mountain, an object they pointed out
as being the bow of Noah's ship.  When Navarra's party
came close to it, they saw that it was not the ark, but
only rock projecting from the side of the mountain. [96]
     Navarra returned in 1955 and saw at the bottom of a
deep crevasse some dark lines in the ice which he thought
were the remains of the ark.  But when he descended to
them, he found that they were only lines of dust and dirt.
(This illustrates the weakness of alleged sightings made
from a distance.)  Nevertheless, when he dug down in the
ice, he happened to find a large, hand-tooled wooden
beam.  He cut off a piece about five feet in length.  The
elevation of this site is about 13,500 feet, and is not the
same location as that of his 1952 "sighting."
     In 1969 Navarra joined the Scientific Exploration and
Archaeological Research (SEARCH) expedition to Mount
Ararat to explore further for the ark.  The snow was not
melted as deeply in the crevasse as in 1955, and the expedition found nothing there.  About 75 feet away they did
find in a lake bottom five pieces of wood, seventeen inches
and less in length.
     The September 5, 1960 issue of _Life_ magazine (pp.
112-14) reproduces an aerial photograph of something
that appears to be the outline of the top deck of a ship.
It is long and narrow, rounded at one end and pointed
at the other.  The location is not Mount Ararat, but a
mountain 20 miles south of it.  The picture was one of
many among official Turkish survey photographs.  While
examining them a Turkish captain noticed that the outline
resembled a ship.  Consequently an expedition was formed,
which included some American scientists.  They found
that the object was only a grassy mound about 500 feet
long and 160 feet wide, surrounded by an earth-packed rim
about 20 feet in height.  The team surveyed it for two days
and took photographs, some of which are reproduced in
the magazine.  The group found that the mound was created by a recent landslide.  The Turkish soldiers who es-
corted the expedition dynamited a section of the rim and

found some "small bits of wood but no large chunks." The scientists concluded that the formation was not caused by any man-made structure, except that one scientist refused to believe that nature could produce such a symmetrical shape.

In 1964 and 1966 the Archaeological Research Foundation carefully surveyed the geological, glaciological, and topographical features of Mount Ararat. Most of the members of the team, which included Eryl Cummings, were stout believers in the historicity of the Flood. One of the photographs of the northern side of the mountain taken by Mr. Cummings in 1966 shows a dark object in a deep canyon; the object could be large rock, but some have interpreted it as possibly the ark. It certainly appears to be a rock in the reproduction in Balsiger and Sellier's book. [97]

SEARCH planned to organize and finance a major expedition that would go to Mount Ararat in 1970. It was to look for remains of the ark, conduct archaeological excavation, and carry out geophysical-glaciological research. The expedition was to have the use of modern equipment for core drilling, infrared photography, and chemical testing. It was prepared to spend as much as one million dollars. The Turkish government, however, revoked its permits, and subsequently has generally refused permission to ark-hunting expeditions. The Soviets charged that the Americans were CIA agents coming to set up equipment to spy on them from the lofty mountain on their border, and the Turks did not want to provoke them. [98] An aspect contributing to suspicion was the fact that it seems incredible to the Russians and the Turks--and to some of the rest of us--that in this modern age some people still believe there was once a Noah's ark. Nevertheless, Montgomery succeeded in obtaining permission in 1970 and 1971.

The Holy Ground Changing Center in Frankston, Texas, possesses a controversial photograph which it contends it took on Mount Ararat in 1974. The Center claims that the photo shows the side of the ark's bow, with the "planking" clearly visible. The picture was one of those shown in the film, "In Search of Noah's Ark," and is reproduced by Balsiger and Sellier.[99] The caption under the picture in the Balsiger and Sellier book admits that some critics contend that the photo is not genuine.

This brief summary of the ascents and explorations of Mount Ararat in hope of finding the ark covers only the better-known, recorded instances. But there have been many others. Gaskill has remarked that in the summer the hotel at the nearby town of Dogubayzit "swarms with Ararat climbers or would-be climbers."[100] Great Ararat has been explored on all sides by ark enthusiasts, and must have been explored considerably also by military units. An impressive number of ascents have been made; Montgomery, in his "Appendix B," lists 17 in the nineteenth century alone. In the twentieth century large sums of money have been spent on organized expeditions to find remains of the ark. Often the public was solicited for funds for the expeditions. Surely the mountain has been searched quite extensively by now!

# CHAPTER 11

## IS THE ARK UP THERE?

"There must be something to it. So many people have said the ark is up there." So said one of my friends when she learned that I was writing this book.

Is there really anything to it? Let's examine the evidence--real and alleged.

## UNRELIABILITY OF ANCIENT TRADITIONS

One of the surprising things about the approach of the eager believers is their trust in ancient traditions. This is manifest not only in their faith in the historical accuracy of stories in the Bible, but also in their confidence in patristic statements and medieval traditions that indicated that the ark was on Mount Ararat.

It is true that Theophilus, Hippolytus, Chrysostom, and Epiphanius stated that remains of the ark still existed and could be seen. They did not agree on where the remains were, however, and they did not claim that they themselves had seen those remains. They were merely incorporating into Christian faith the pagan and Jewish idea that wherever the ship landed, it could still be seen there. Many, many other patristic traditions have proved to be erroneous. The church fathers lacked an accurate knowledge of history. For the sake of promoting their beliefs, they even changed the text of the Bible sometimes when they quoted it.

Especially during the Middle Ages many superstitions and unreliable traditions arose. The Armenian Christians in the region of Mount Ararat contributed their fair share of legends. Here are some samples. [101]

1. The Garden of Eden had been in the Araxes Valley

below Mount Ararat.

2.  The tomb of Noah was shown nearby.

3.  An ancient vine stock, still bearing grapes, at the foot of the mountain was pointed out to Bryce as one that Noah had planted.  God had forbidden that wine be made from its grapes, because they had caused Noah's drunkenness.

4.  Before the birth of Jesus, twelve wise men stood by a pillar on the top of the mountain and watched for his star to appear.  When it did, three of them followed it to Bethlehem [a long trek!].

5.  The spring on the side of the Ahora Gorge first burst forth when Saint Jacob laid his head on the ground there when he prayed.

6.  The villagers at Arghuri showed an ancient willow trunk, which they said sprang from a plank of Noah's ark.

7.  The monastery of Saint Jacob, or Saint James, was claimed to be on the very spot where the angel had appeared to Saint Jacob.

8.  When crops are threatened by locusts, a bottle of water from Jacob's Well, if placed in the field, will attract the tetagush bird, which will devour the locusts and save the crops.  The bottle must not be allowed to touch the ground, however, while it is being carried from the well to the field.

The fanciful nature of these legends should alert us to the danger of taking seriously another Ararat legend: that of the ark on the mountain.


RELICS

The possession of religious relics was another practice that was characteristic of the Middle Ages.  Churches and monasteries tried to surpass one another in the merits of their sacred objects; therefore more and more extravagant claims were made.  Relics were carefully pro-

tected in taffeta wrappings and reliquaries.  The relics
varied from the numerous alleged pieces of the cross on
which Jesus was crucified to John the Baptist's thumb.

Carveth Wells encountered a tradition about the coat
of Jesus at the Cathedral Church of the Twelve Apostles
in the village of Mtzkhet, near Tiflis in the Soviet Union.
Bishop Alexis, who was in charge of the church, showed
him the shrine in which it was kept, but would not show
him the coat.  According to legend, a Jew from that
town was present at Jesus' crucifixion, and he purchased
the coat from the soldier who won it when the soldiers
cast lots for Jesus' clothing.  After bringing it home, he
gave it to his sister Sidonia, but as soon as she put it on,
she fell dead.  Years later, the place of her burial was
revealed in a dream, and her body was dug up.  Because
she was wearing the coat, her body was perfectly preserved and emitted a delightful fragrance.  The coat has
been preserved ever since, they say, in the church as a
holy relic. [102]

The Armenian Christian monastery at Echmiadzin,
too, acquired holy relics.  Like many other churches
and monasteries, it purported to have a piece of Jesus'
cross and some nails from the cross.  Its monks also
said that the monastery had the iron spear which was
thrust into Jesus' side; the spear was brought to the
church by none other than the apostle Thaddeus himself.
[But Thaddeus was a disciple of Jesus in the first century, while the monastery was not founded until the
fourth century--A. D.  302, according to tradition. ]  And
OF COURSE the monastery had a piece of Noah's ark as
its most valued holy relic--the very piece that an angel
had given to Saint Jacob! [103]  At this monastery both
Friedrich Parrot in 1829 and Carveth Wells in 1932 were
shown a relic claimed to be a piece of the ark.  When the
two descriptions are compared with each other, the two
two relics appear to be different pieces of wood: a small
piece of natural wood vs. a larger piece of petrified
wood. [104]

As we saw in chapter 10, the tradition that Saint Jacob brought a piece of the wood down the mountain is a story that goes back to the fourth century and was quite prevalent in the Middle Ages. We saw, too, that other purported relics made from the ark were current in the seventeenth century: at Ararat (Struys) and at Schamachy in Persia (Olearius).

## LOCATION AND SHAPE OF THE ARK

The precise location of the ark has often been a problem for the ark believers. To this day, some believe that it is, or at least once was, on a different mountain, Mount Judi. Nevertheless, for centuries most Christians believed that if the ark still existed, it was on the top of Mount Ararat.

After explorers ascended Ararat in the nineteenth century and found nothing but ice and snow, two different views developed: either the ark is still on the summit under the ice, or it has slid down part way and, hopefully, may be found in a glacier on the slopes. Explorers lost interest in the first view, for it offered little hope or excitement and could not be investigated. Various alleged "sightings" of the ark occurred on the slopes, and assorted pieces of wood were found there and considered to be part of the ark. It is significant that as long as men were confident that the ark was on the summit, no one saw it or its remains on the slopes. After hope in the summit was lost, however, "sightings" and wood suddenly appeared on the slopes!

In fact, sightings and wood appeared in many places-- too many places! Admittedly, if there were an ark, the "broken ark" theory would be plausible. This is the theory that the ark is no longer in one piece, but broken into several. But would it be scattered so widely in so many places? Even when the same explorer returns, he does not find wood again in the same place.

Speaking of location, here is another problem.  Although the ark is presumed to have landed on the top of Great Ararat and to have remained up there for centuries, local tradition asserts that Noah discharged the animals from the ark on Kip Göl, or Kip Ghioll, the plain near Lake Kop.  The altitude of the plain is about 12,000 feet.  Now if that local tradition is true, how did the ark get back to the top again?  Or if the ark stayed on the plain, why look for it above that altitude?  Since the plain is below the permanent glaciers, the ark should be clearly visible in the summertime--if it is still there. And if the ark believers assert that they do not believe this local tradition, may we ask: Why believe that other local tradition (at least it originated as a local tradition), namely, the tradition that the ark is on Mount Ararat? What is their basis for accepting one tradition and not the other?

One of the inconsistencies in the "evidence" for the ark is that the so-called sightings do not agree on the shape of the ark.  In the Bible the shape is that of a rectangular box, and some climbers have thought that they have seen that form, or at least a flat side or a rectangular end.  On the other hand, some climbers have seen regular boat shapes, with curved sides, as Navarra did in 1952.

## THE WOOD

The search for the ark has gone through interesting cycles.  At first the search was for the whole ark (F. Parrot); next, a stick on the surface was regarded as good evidence (Bryce); then the claims reverted to the whole ark (Nouri, Roskovitsky); while in recent decades the main interest and hope has been in digging up wood. When twentieth century explorers found wood, cut off a chunk, and claimed that they had a piece of the ark, their claims remind us, somehow, of the earlier claims of possessing relics made from wood which some monk said he had personally cut from the ark.

Whenever eager believers find old wood on Great Ararat, they usually assume that it comes from the ark. They conveniently overlook the other possible sources. But other possibilities there are, sources far more probable than the ark.

Professor Lloyd R. Bailey has aptly remarked that "not only have wood fragments been carried down the mountain for investigation, but a considerable amount of wood has been carried up it in recent times as well."[105] Very true, and it is not just in recent times that wood has been carried up Great Ararat, as Bailey recognizes. From the Middle Ages to modern times men who traveled on the mountain took firewood with them on donkeys' backs, for cooking and for heat. More important, hermits and peasants living on the slopes took up timbers of considerable size to use in building their huts, as well as smaller sticks for firewood. As we have seen, in the nineteenth century F. Parrot, Abich, and Khodzko carried up wooden crosses to plant on the summit. When Bryce found a stick, he realized that it could have been carried up, but he was reluctant to admit it. It is true that most of this wood was not carried all the way up to the summit, but searchers have abandoned hope of finding ark remains at the top anyway. Wood was probably carried up in very ancient times too, for huts and firewood. Thus even if wood 5,000 years old were found on the mountain, it would not necessarily be from any ark.

The condition or nature of the "ark wood" found on Mount Ararat fails to follow a consistent pattern. Some of the wood seems to be in natural condition so that it can be cut and split; some of it is petrified, which is rock and cannot be cut like wood; some is reported to be soft and soggy. Could such a variety all be wood from the ark? The alleged ark wood was not consistent in its condition in the seventeenth century either. According to Olearius,

the wood was petrified, while according to the hermit
monk reported by Struys, it was still soft enough for him
to cut off a piece from the ark and shape it into a cross.
The argument used to defend the inconsistency in the nature of the wood is that there must have been different
conditions in different parts of the mountain, so that
some of the wood became petrified and some did not.
The argument is based on conjecture, not evidence or
scientific probabilities.

The age of the "ark wood" has become a controversial issue in recent years, for the ark enthusiasts regard
the antiquity of the wood as vital evidence. They assume
that if the wood is old enough, it must have come from
the ark. Nevertheless, that assumption does not satisfy
the skeptics. The wood that Navarra found in 1955 and
1969 has been tested for age. Only his wood has been
tested, because his is the only "ark wood" available.

At first Navarra's 1955 wood was analyzed only by
old methods. The Forestry Institute of Research and
Experimentation in Madrid tested it in 1956 and concluded that it was white oak, about 5,000 years old. The Department of Anthropology and Prehistoric Studies at the
University of Bordeaux, France, set no date, but concluded that the wood came from "great antiquity." Such
dating is just what the ark believers like to hear. Wood
that was 5,000 years old in 1955 would give us a date of
origin of about 3,050 B.C. This fits only loosely the old
dating of the Flood by Ussher (2,348 B.C.; to really fit,
the wood should have been about 4,300 years old). The
tests were based on color, density changes, cell degra-
dation, and the degree of lignitization and fossilization.
All these criteria are questionable, however, and are
discussed at length by Bailey.[106]

The radiocarbon method now used by scientists, on
the other hand, is a reliable method of dating ancient organic material. Willard F. Libby at the University of
Chicago discovered it around 1950. The rate at which
organic materials lose their carbon 14 content is now

known. Therefore, by burning a sample of the matter and measuring the amount of carbon 14 in it, the age of that material can be determined within 100 years or less back to 20,000 to 30,000 years ago. In the 1960s five reputable laboratories conducted the carbon 14 test on samples of the wood Navarra found in 1955: the National Physical Laboratory in England, and the University of California at Los Angeles and at Riverside, the Geochron Laboratories, and Teledyne Isotopes in the United States. Three of these laboratories dated the wood in the eighth century A.D.; one differed from that date by "a couple of centuries"; one dated it in the third century A.D. In the 1970s two laboratories, Geochron Laboratories and the University of Pennsylvania Radiocarbon Laboratory, applied the carbon 14 test to the wood Navarra found in 1969; both arrived at a date around A.D. 640. Thus none of the wood existed in Old Testament times. [107]

Needless to say, the ark enthusiasts do not like the results of the carbon 14 tests, which demonstrate that Navarra's wood cannot possibly be from the ark; they have been relying on this wood to support their claims. Therefore they have striven to discredit the carbon 14 test. They have argued that the results differ from each other too much, that the high elevation of the wood on the mountain might slow down the rate of discharge of carbon 14, and that the wood may have been contaminated by water soluble carbon 14. If these conditions existed, they would interfere with the accuracy of the test. As for the first charge, three of the tests of the 1955 wood do agree within 40 years, and the amount of the sample was insufficient in the test that indicated a third century A.D. date. The tests of the 1969 wood fully agree with each other. Careful testing has shown that the other two charges against the carbon 14 test are not true either. [108] The validity of the test has often been confirmed by other evidence; for example, by coins in the case of the Dead Sea scrolls. The actual basis of the futile effort to discredit the carbon 14 test was zeal to defend belief in the

ark.  Recently the test has been improved further by sep-
arating carbon 14 and carbon 12, and then comparing the
ratio of the two types of carbons.  With this method earlier dates can be determined. [109]


PHOTOGRAPHS

A characteristic of many of the photographs of the ark
is that, for some reason or other, they cannot be seen.
They have been  "lost, " or they "belong to the Soviet government, " or they cannot be released "for security reasons. "  This pattern arouses the suspicion that some of
them never existed in the first place.

A characteristic of the few that can be seen is that
they are vague and look much more like ordinary rock
than like an ark (whether petrified or not).  Cummings'
photo taken during the 1966 Archaeological Research Foundation's expedition--as reproduced in Balsiger and Sellier's book at least--is indistinct and looks like a chunk of
rock.  The telephoto shot taken (or claimed to have been
taken) by the Holy Ground Changing Center in 1974 is alleged to show "planking. "  It is reproduced in Balsiger
and Sellier's book and in the film, "In Search of Noah's
Ark. "  Some of us think that it merely looks like layers
of stratified rock.  It may be even less than that.  The
caption under the reproduction in the book admits that
some people have charged that the photograph has been
retouched.

Aerial photographs deserve a special comment.  Usually they are taken from such a distance that they do not
show sufficient detail.  Also, earth formations seen from
the air can look like ships, as the formation on another
mountain (reported in Life, Sept. 5, 1960) illustrates.


SCIENTISTS

Ark enthusiasts, like fundamentalists in general, have difficulty in deciding whether they are for or against science, and for or against scientists. When a scientist makes a statement they can use to support their views, they gladly cite him as a scientist. They often regard their own views as "scientific." The Balsiger and Sellier book furnishes examples. Genuine geologists do not believe there was a universal flood, but the book tries to connect geologists with the belief by using the expression "flood geologists." The book often states that "scientists" or "many scientists" believe things that would support the ark enthusiasts' views [whether any scientists in the field believe these things is doubtful, and it is certain that scientists generally do not]. Thus in these statements science is held in honor and there is an effort to identify with it.

But when scientists disagree with their views, the ark people tend to disparage scientists in general. The film states that about a century ago science began to question Genesis by saying that it consists of myths and legends; then the film tries to refute that view by defending the historicity of the Flood and Noah's ark. The implication is that science was wrong. A bizarre example of smearing scientists is the wild story reportedly told by Haji Yearam, an Armenian who migrated to America. According to the story, when Yearam was a boy in Armenia, three vile scientists, who did not believe in God and the Bible, came to Mount Ararat to disprove the story of Noah's ark. They hired the boy and his father to guide them. The Yearams led them up to the ark near the top of the mountain. The scientists were so angry at finding the ark that they vainly tried to destroy it. Then they vowed that if Yearam and his father ever told anyone that the ark was there, the scientists would torture and murder them! The story has been circulated widely among ark enthusiasts, and apparently some of them believe it. It is reported in the film that was televised nationally and is in Balsiger and Sellier's

book. [110] The hostility to scientists that is behind this
ridiculous story is quite obvious.


## IS IT THERE?

When asked if the ark would ever be found, Froelich
Rainey, the director of the University Museum at the University of Pennsylvania, reportedly remarked that "if
there's anything that's impossible in archaeology, this
is it." [111]

Our examination of the "evidence" for an ark on
Mount Ararat finds that none of it is valid. If that is not
convincing enough, we should remember this: the ark
never existed in the first place.

At the conclusion of the film, "In Search of Noah's
Ark," the narrator, remarks, "The ark is there."

Quite the contrary.
The ark is not there.
AND IT NEVER WAS!

The ark enthusiasts should take seriously the cartoon
in The New Yorker (November 27, 1971), which Montgomery reproduced in his book. [112] The cartoon shows a man
walking up a mountain, and the farther he goes, the
steeper it becomes. Finally he comes to a sign which
reads "THINK." He does exactly that; he turns around
and walks back down the mountain.

The ark people should follow his example. They
should stop and think, turn around, and give up the
attempt.

# CHAPTER 12

## THE MEDIA

Why has the belief in Noah's ark on Mount Ararat been promoted so vigorously, in spite of the lack of any solid evidence for it? We have already discussed one cause: religious fundamentalism. There is another major cause, however: sensationalism. Some authors, media people, and advertisers have found that sensational material can be very profitable.

Such material would not be quite so bad if all the essential facts pertaining to the subject were presented, and presented accurately, with a clear distinction between fact and fiction maintained. But that is rarely the case with sensational material.

Sensationalism as a major interest is not new in magazines, books, and newspapers. Nor is it new in films or even television. The horror films of the 1930s and 1940s, such as the Frankenstein movies, have been replaced by the scare films of the 1960s amd 1970s, such as "Earthquake," "Jaws," and "Swarm." Some of these films arouse unhealthy fears, [113] but at least they are presented as fiction. Then came television, and it, too, yielded to the temptation to use sensationalism. In recent years a new, especially dangerous, form has appeared: the sensational pseudo-documentary film or television program.

Three types of books, films, and programs appear to be documentaries. First, there is the genuine documentary, an accurate report founded on careful research. The documentary may take a position on an issue, but it is fair to all sides, and its conclusions are reached after objective study. Its evidence in genuine and its reasoning sound. Edwin Newman's program, "Land of Hype and Glory," is an excellent example.

A second category of documentary is the "faction," a term that Alex Haley is reported to have applied to his book, Roots. The faction is a mixture of fact and fiction. It enables readers and viewers to recognize that it contains some fiction, and the fictitious elements are included in order to give a clearer understanding of history or the nature of the subject.

The third category is the pseudo documentary. It purports to be a genuine documentary, and on the surface appears to be an objective, factual investigation of a subject. Actually, the pseudo documentary is not the result of objective research, it omits part of the evidence, may misinterpret some of the evidence it does present, and aims to promote a certain idea at the expense of a different view, usually in a sensational manner.

An early specimen of the pseudo documentary, shown on television, was the program based on Erich von Däniken's book, Chariots of the Gods. The book was widely read, and its theory believed by some people. Fortunately, the theory has been refuted in a recent book by Ronald Story.[114] The theory of the program is that very intelligent visitors from outer space came to the earth and left their mark, both physically and culturally. The film presents the theory in a documentary fashion, showing archaeological features, one after another, which supposedly indicate that in the distant past "gods" came to earth in spaceships. Archaeologists' interpretations of the material are often omitted, and much other archaeological evidence is not mentioned.

Another presentation in the pseudo documentary category was "Madness and Medicine," televised by ABC May 26, 1977. The American Psychiatric Association filed a formal complaint against it with the Federal Communication Commission, charging that it was "a one-sided attack on psychiatry," which did not present opposing views and seemed to be "a broad condemnation of psychiatry in general." The program gave me that impression too. The program criticized psychiatrists' use of drug therapy, electroconvulsive therapy, and psychosurgery, but did not consider the numerous cases where those methods have had benficial effects, nor did it make sufficiently clear that psychiatry is a far larger field than those methods.[115]


## IN SEARCH OF NOAH'S ARK

The film, "In Search of Noah's Ark," is also in the pseudo-documentary category; although the format is that of a historical investigation, the views of historians generally are omitted. It was telecast by NBC in the summer of 1977 and again on Christmas Eve of the same year. It was produced by Sun Classic Pictures, Inc., and the book by the same name was published by its subsidiary, Sun Classic Books. There is a close connection between the film and the book. Sun Classic Pictures copyrighted the book.[116] Sun Classic Pictures has produced other sensational films such as "Ghosts from the Dead" and "The Lincoln Conspiracy"; the latter was televised by NBC in prime time May 16, 1978. When "The Lincoln Conspiracy" was telecast, the program began with a statement that the film presents the producer's theory, and that his theory is at odds with many traditional views of the subject.

Let us take a look at the nature of the film, "In Search of Noah's Ark." First, its content, and second, its technique.

The film began by trying to establish that archaeology has shown that the Bible is true. At best, that claim is only a half-truth. Actually, archaeology provides support for some statements, and evidence against other statements in the Bible. The ziggurat in Babylon was pointed out in the film as proof of the existence of the Tower of Babel mentioned in Genesis 11. The basis of the Genesis account, however, is not knowledge of an event in Babylon, but a Hebrew adaptation of a Babylonian

account--discovered through archaeology--of its founding of the city of Babylon. In the Babylonain source men
are not trying to build a tower up to the heavens, but a
temple with its top pointed toward the sky. [117] Also, in
the Babylonian original, building the city and the ziggurat
do not result in the confusion of human language, as it
does in Genesis. Thus the effect of archaeology on the
story in Genesis 11 is to disprove the Bible as history;
like the story of the Flood in Genesis, the Tower of Babel
story in the same book is an adaptation to Hebrew religion
of an ancient Mesopotamian account. The film then mentioned that archaeologists have found that Jericho was un-
occupied for a period of time, which agrees with the Bible
[Joshua 6:26]. This archaeological evidence does not
verify the details of the fall of Jericho, however, though
it does illustrate the incorporation of some factual knowledge into the biblical accounts.

The film finishes the first section by having the narrator say, "Genesis is a remarkable historical document,
and the story of Noah is in it." Now the logic unfolds! The
reasoning is: archaeology has shown that the Bible is true;
Genesis is in the Bible and therefore is true; the story of
Noah is in Genesis and therefore is true. But the argumen
is not sound. The fallacy of the logic is that archaeology
has not shown that the whole Bible is true [in fact, archaeology and other evidence have shown that parts of the
Bible, including parts of Genesis, are not true], and
therefore the fact that the story of Noah is in Genesis does
not prove the historicity of the story at all. Incidentally,
the story about Jericho is in the book of Joshua, not Genesis, so it does not and could not demonstrate that Genesis
is a historical document.

Next, the film's narrator stated that about a century
ago science began to question Genesis and say that it consists of myths and legends. Some persons, the narrator
continued, have disagreed with the scientists and have
maintained that Genesis is history. These persons are,
"historians, archaeologists, scholars." This statement

introduced the other two sections of the film: an effort
to show that the Flood could have occurred, and a survey
of the attempts to find Noah's ark on Mount Ararat.

The film ended not only with the remark that "the
ark is there," but also with the conclusion that the story
of Noah's ark is "impeccably true." Judging from the
introduction to the film, that conclusion implies that the
whole Bible, too, is completely true. Thus the film not
only tries to persuade the audience that the ark is there,
but also that the Bible as a whole is literally true--the
latter is the doctrine of religious fundamentalism.

The technique employed in the film is that of the
pseudo documentary. The format is that of an objective,
factual investigation, with the narrator raising questions,
exhibiting (alleged) evidence, and interviewing (alleged)
authorities. But the film is not based on an objective,
factual investigation. The real authorities on the subject
are not interviewed. It omits evidence against its arguments; the evidence it does give will not stand up under
examination. It erroneously presents its views as those
of historians and archaeologists. The film did not mention the fact that its thesis has long been rejected by the
seminaries of mainline churches and by the religion and
history departments of nearly all colleges and universi-
ties in the Western world. Nor did it tell the viewers
that its claim that the Flood actually occurred is contrary
to the interpretation of the Bible in the standard commentaries on Genesis. In short, the technique in the film is
to misuse a documentary format.


NETWORK COMPETITION

Commercial television began with a moderate sense
of responsibility to the public, guided to some extent by
precedents from radio broadcasting. Policies of the Federal Communications Commission developed the sense of
responsibility, and major advances resulted from the

work of Fred W. Friendly and Edward R. Murrow.

Nevertheless, television networks are business cor-
porations, with boards and stockholders expecting con-
stantly increasing profits. In the last few years the pres-
sures have increased and the competition has become
fierce. The effect upon the programs has been serious
enough to attract the attention of critics and cause a de-
cline in the number of viewers. [118] Profits in television
depend on income from advertising; income from advertising depends on the amount of air time sold and the
amount charged for it; the advertising time and rate
charged depend largely on each network's Nielsen ratings.
These ratings are based on the estimated number of viewers watching particular shows. In the Nielsen system
the national ratings are based on only 1200 homes whose
television sets are connected with computers.

According to various published reports, the pattern
among the big three (ABC, CBS, NBC) runs like this:
The network board demands that the network officials, or
managers, present programs with high ratings (hopefully
higher than the ratings of their competitors or those of
their own shows the previous season); since "junk" tends
to rate the highest, managers must choose that kind of
program or be fired; many submit, but some stand by
their standards and take the consequences. Occasionally
there are exceptions to the rule that junk rates best;
"Roots" was an excellent, constructive program which
led in the ratings.

Numerous television producers, writers, and managers have expressed their disapproval of the situation.
Norman Lear is quoted as saying that competition is "the
most destructive force in television today."[119] TV Guide
reported that Universal-TV's president, Frank Price, remarked that if there were less emphasis on ratings and
less urge to make "greater and greater profits," the networks might "feel a little more free to put on something
they thought was good."[120] Steve Allen has said that much
of television is "junk food for the mind."[121] Many lo-

cal station managers are of the same opinion, but are obliged to broadcast what the networks provide. Admittedly, some very good programs are presented too, but they are far too few compared with those that could be and should be available to the viewer. A recent encouraging development, however, is the ABC decision to produce documentaries of superior quality.[122]

## REI'S COMPLAINT

When one wonders why NBC telecast nationally such a film as "In Search of Noah's Ark, " the only plausible reason is that NBC was trying to raise its ratings (it trailed behind both ABC and CBS at the time) by showing something sensational. The film was shown in the "NBC Movie" series. For about a week before the Christmas Eve broadcast, NBC publicized its forthcoming presentation of the film by showing, at least twice, a spot advertisement on its stations. As I recall, the impression was given in these brief commercials that the film was documentary. In the "Movie Index" of tv news (in the Chicago Daily News, Dec. 24) for December 24-31, 1977, the film is classified as a "documentary drama" (p. 36).

With my professional training in ancient history and biblical scholarship, I knew that Noah's ark is not on Mount Ararat because Noah's ark never existed in the first place. Therefore, with pencil and paper in hand, I monitored the telecast. The film was even worse than I had feared.

If the reader has never filed a complaint, he or she may be interested in knowing the steps involved. First, one should write a letter to the network (if the program is national). If no reply is received within thirty days, or if the reply is unsatisfactory, write a letter of complaint to the Federal Communications Commission (no special form is necessary).

As Executive Director of the Religion and Ethics Institute, I wrote to the TV Program Director of the National Broadcasting Company in New York, protesting the program, and charging that it was "irresponsible broadcasting." A copy of the letter was sent to FCC in Washington. FCC sent us a copy of its informational memorandum on policy concerning the Fairness Doctrine and procedures to follow in filing complaints. A lengthy report on the Fairness Doctrine was attached to the memorandum; the report had been printed in the <u>Federal Register</u> in 1974.[123] In my letter I registered some objections to the film, then asked NBC to:

> a. present no more propaganda films disguised as objective reports of objective investigations.
> b. present nationwide at least thirty (30) minutes in the same prime time (9-11 PM EST) the case against the historicity of the story of Noah and the ark and against the existence of the ark on Mt. Ararat.

After waiting in vain for a month and a half for a reply to the letter, I addressed a formal complaint, in behalf of REI (the Religion and Ethics Institute) to FCC. Then NBC suddenly awoke and directed my original letter to its Law Department. Mr. William T. Abbott, Senior Counsel of the department, wrote to apologize for NBC's failure to respond promptly to our letter, which he stated "was originally misdirected within NBC," and that NBC was preparing a response. The response, written on March 9 by Mr. Abbott, briefly stated NBC's defense of its telecast.

Dissatisfied with the response, we filed on March 14 the formal complaint with FCC, which promptly sent a form letter to NBC, requesting that it respond to the complaint within ten days or give the reasons for not doing so. The form letter added these directions:

> If the complainant is not satisfied with your

response and wishes to submit comments on
it, complainant should file such comments,
in duplicate, within seven days of receipt of
your response. Should no comments be received from the complainant, it will be assumed the complainant does not wish to take
issue with the licensee's response. In either
event, the Commission will then determine
what action, if any, is appropriate in light of
the information before it.

On March 27 NBC's Senior Attorney in Washington,
John F. Sturm, gave NBC's reply to FCC, a reply that
was a brief restatement of Mr. Abbott's response. We
did not send comments on it to FCC, for we felt that we
had already covered the points. On May 18 Arthur L.
Ginsburg, Acting Chief of the Complaints and Compliance
Division, Broadcast Bureau, FCC, replied to REI and
essentially agreed with NBC's position. Mr. Ginsburg's
letter stated that the Commission [FCC] had concluded
that "the program did not discuss a controversial issue
of public importance, and no Commission action is war-
ranted on your complaint." His letter added that this
was a staff action, and then it outlined the procedure if
REI wished to apply for Review by the full Commission.
We did not pursue the complaint further, for we felt that
with the refusal of NBC and FCC ro recognize the really
significant issues involved and with their devious interpretation of the law, the cards were stacked against the
complaint.

## THE ARGUMENTS

### REI's Case

A. The film advances an obsolete interpretation of
the Bible, namely, the belief that the Flood story in Gen-

esis is historical and that a universal Flood actually occurred.

   1.   This interpretation is refuted by the evidence,
set forth in this book in the section entitled "The Flood."

   2.   The interpretation is rejected by the seminaries of mainline churches, the main Jewish seminaries,
and the departments of religion of all colleges and univer-
sities, except the fundamentalist and the more conservative of the evangelical schools.

   3.   The interpretation is rejected in virtually all
standard commentaries on Genesis or on the Bible.

   B.   The film does not present "the other side," the
case against its own interpretation of the Flood story,
even though the other side is recognized by scholars in
the field as the correct view.   The film generally uses
the tactic of omitting the abundant evidence against the
historicity of the story.   For example, it did not present
the similar Mesopotamian Flood stories which are earlier and are the ultimate sources of the biblical version.
This tactic is incongruous with the film's framework,
which is that of an objective investigation.   Both the content and the technique of the film violate the principles of
scholarship.

   C.   The film's theme that Noah's ark is on Mount Ararat is a view that is untenable, even ridiculous.   The alleged evidence is flimsy at best and false at worst, as
shown in "The Ark" section of this book.   The evidence
against the theme is conveniently neglected.

   D.   The film sets forth its view as that of "historians, archaeologists, scholars," and did not mention the
fact that historians, archaeologists, and scholars generally reject the film's view.   The film misled some of the
public into believing that the point of view of these categories of people is the opposite of what it really is.   I
know the film had this effect, for I have talked with people
who were persuaded by it.

   E.   The film does not even report the biblical Flood
story accurately.   The narrator explains that Noah's fam-

ily was able to get all those animals on board because God had spoken to the animals and they came willingly. This nonsense is not in the Bible. And the film does not report that two different versions of the Flood story, from two different periods of time, are combined in the Genesis account.

F. The film is sectarian propaganda, for it tries to show in typical fundamentalist fashion that the Bible is true. It is not an accident that the film begins with the claim that archaeology has shown that "the Bible is true." Only from a fundamentalist perspective does the film's conclusion make any sense, namely the statement that "Noah is our link to the past and our hope for the future." The main concern of the film really is not an investigation of whether or not the ark is on Mount Ararat. The film's chief interest is to persuade the audience that: the ark is up there, and therefore the story of Noah is true, and therefore the Bible is true. The implication is that therefore the fundamentalist interpretation of the Bible is true, contrary to the interpretation of most of the rest of us. It is significant that the film presented the same "evidence" and the same arguments, often in the same order, as the various fundamentalist books that try to persuade readers that the ark is on Ararat. The order in the film and books is: (1) the Bible is true; (2) the Flood really happened; (3) history of the attempts to find the ark on Mount Ararat; (4) the ark must be up there. The effort to use archaeology as support for fundamentalism is also typical.

G. "The most dangerous aspect of the whole presentation was its pretense of being an objective investigation, presented as a documentary, when actually it was religious sectarian propaganda. . . . The tactic of disguising propaganda as objective investigations is an insidious device that opens the way for all sorts of 'brainwashing' of the public." Thus I wrote in REI's formal complaint to FCC. The device could be used for all sorts of subjects--not just religion, but political issues, economic issues, and

social issues.  When such films are telecast nationally,
the influence is widespread.  When FCC is blind to the
danger, the potential for thought control is enormous.
The device is a hindrance to the dissemination of scholarship, a threat to the public's right to know the facts,
and a menace to intellectual progress in society.

H.  Considering the nature of the film, NBC should
not have selected it for showing.  Admittedly, the film
had been shown in some theaters, and NBC presented it
as a movie in its "NBC Movie" series.  Nevertheless,
the film has a documentary format, and NBC should have
recognized the sectarian nature of the film, the flimsiness
of its evidence, and its unfairness to scientists and to genuine historians, archaeologists, and biblical scholars.
The film is unfair to scientists by implying that their interpretation of the Bible is wrong, and it is unfair to the
genuine historians, archaeologists, and scholars by implying that their view of the story of the Flood and Noah's
ark is the opposite of what it really is.

### NBC's Case

The presentation of NBC's case is unavoidably brief,
because the response of its attorneys, Mr. Abbott and
Mr. Sturm, is brief in their letters.  If we were to expand on their statements, we might ascribe to them
thoughts they did not have.  The quotations below are
from their letters and from mine to FCC on 3/14/78.

A.  NBC did not act "irresponsibly in presenting
this program." (Abbott).  The program was only entertainment, and NBC did not act irresponsibly in telecast-
ing it.

Rebuttal.  The program was not mere entertainment, but sectarian propaganda as well.

B.  "NBC promoted and presented the film as entertainment, not as news or religious programming.  In this
regard, we made certain that there would not be viewer
confusion by including the following advisory:

'The following program is intended as an
entertaining look at a subject surrounded
in mystery and speculation.  In part the
information presented is based on theory
and conjecture and not on established fact.'" (Abbott)

Rebuttal.  There is no doubt that NBC's intent, in
contrast to that of the film, was merely entertainment.
The advisory apparently had little effect, however, for
everyone I have talked with who saw the film, had the impression that the film was a serious effort to persuade
the audience that "the Bible is true," the story of Noah
is "impeccably true," and "the ark is there."  This
telecast illustrates the worthlessness of an advisory, or
disclaimer preceding programs.  Some viewers acci-
dentally miss the advisory by not watching the program
at the moment it is shown.  (I started viewing this program about 30 seconds late and did not see the advisory).
Other viewers disregard the disclaimer and are taken in
by the program anyway, as happened with this film.

C.   The viewers were not "misled regarding the program's intent" (Abbott).  The "intent" was entertainment
(if I understand Mr. Abbott's letter correctly).

Rebuttal.  Although NBC's intent admittedly was
only entertainment, the program's effect was the foster-
ing of a sectarian view along with the entertainment.
Viewers were misled on several things; on the views of
historians and archaeologists generally, on the interpretation of the Bible, and on the evidence concerning the
Flood and Noah's ark.

D.   The film did not deal "in any way with controversial issues of public importance" (Abbott), and therefore
NBC is not obligated to present the other side of the question.

Also, in our judgment, the film did not
contain a discussion of any controversial
issue of public importance, nor did it advocate any position on such issues.  Whether or not Noah's ark physically exists is

not in our judgment a controversial issue
of public importance under the fairness
doctrine (Sturm).

Rebuttal. The question of the existence of the ark
on Mount Ararat is not the only issue in the film. The
question of whether the Bible is true is a deep concern of
the film, and that question is a controversial issue of
public importance. How can it be argued that the film did
not advocate a position on that question when the position
is stated so firmly at the beginning ("the Bible is true")
and the whole film builds support for it? Did the NBC
attorneys see the film? Are they familiar with fundamentalism?

E.   The question of the interpretation of the Bible is
not a controversial issue of public importance.

In his most recent letter to the Commission, dated March 14, 1978, Mr. Teeple
raised a number of questions which he
feels were dealt with in the film.   Specif-
ically, he mentions the debate in the Missouri Lutheran Synod over the fundamentalist versus the historical approach to
Bible study.   This debate was not addressed in the film, and even if it were,
we do not believe that the fairness doctrine would impose an obligation on us
to present all of the points of view involved in that debate (Sturm).

Rebuttal.
The fundamentalist approach vs. the historical approach to the Bible is an ex-
tremely controversial issue.   It is the
chief issue between the mainline churches
and many sectarian denominations, between the "Bible schools" and the main
seminaries.   It is the issue which in recent years split the Missouri Synod
Lutheran Church.   IF THIS ISSUE IS NOT

CONTROVERSIAL, WHAT IS? The program presented only one side of the issue
(Teeple, 3/14/78).

F. As for the argument that NBC should present the
other side, "we have provided coverage over the years in
both our religious and news programming" (Abbott).

Rebuttal.

I am a regular viewer of NBC programs,
and I have never seen any program of
theirs which told the real origin of the
flood story or mentioned any books such
as that by the archaeologist André Parrot which refuted the claims that the ark
is on Mount Ararat. If NBC has presented such a program within recent
years, let them provide the evidence
(Teeple, 3/14/78).

If any of the big three television networks has ever
presented a full program of the other side of either the ark
question or the fundamentalist position, I have never seen
it nor heard of it. Even if one was presented five years ago,
that would not adequately balance the current presentation.


COMMENT

Neither NBC nor FCC dealt with some of the tenets in
REI's case. There was no reponse to our charges that an
erroneous impression was given of the views of historians,
archaeologists, and scholars generally; that the film promoted a discredited interpretation of the Bible, an interpretation generally rejected by authorities in the field; and
that the documentary format was misused to promote a
sectarian view.

## THE LAW

It is generally assumed that the law and FCC provide
the public with considerable protection in respect to television programs. We must confess that we have found this
experience rather disillusioning. The law is inadequate,
and FCC's interpretation of it leaves too many loopholes.
The law should be revised, and surely FCC could do more
to raise the standards of television programming. Incidentally, FCC has come under severe criticism recently.[124]

### Summary

Some important features of the law, described in FCC's
"Fairness Doctrine and Public Interest Standards," need
to be kept in mind. FCC's fairness doctrine is especially
concerned with broadcast journalism and is limited to "controversial issues of public importance." What is a controversial issue? One that is "the subject of vigorous debate with substantial elements of the community in opposition to one another." The controversy need not have preceded the program, however, but may arise as the result
of the program. What is an issue of public importance?
FCC's criteria are: (1) the principle test is "a subjective
evaluation of the impact that the issue is likely to have on
the community at large"; (2) "the degree of media coverage" given it; and (3) "the degree of attention the issue
has received from government officials and other community leaders."

According to the law, if the issue is a controversial
one of public importance, the licensee (i.e., the broadcaster) "has a duty to play a conscious and positive role
in encouraging the presentation of opposing viewpoints."
If the broadcaster cannot find a sponsor to pay the cost of
presenting contrasting viewpoints, he should provide the
forum at his own expense. Difficulty in finding a spokes-
man does not release him from his duty. "The mechanics

of achieving fairness will necessarily vary with the cir-
cumstances," however.  Although the licensee should provide a "reasonable opportunity" for the presentation of
opposing views, he need not provide equal time, except
in the case of political broadcasting.  Nevertheless, there
should be a balance in respect to the weight of presentation, taking into consideration prime time vs. non-prime
time, frequency of presentation, and size of listening
audience.  ". . . the fairness doctrine does not require
that each program present contrasting views on an issue;
only that a licensee in its overall programming afford
reasonable opportunity for presentation of contrasting
views."

"As a matter of general procedure, we do not moni-
tor broadcasts for possible violations, but act on the basis of complaints received from interested citizens."
The process of a review of a complaint is as follows:
". . . the Commission's first task in handling a typical
fairness complaint is to review the licensee's determination as to whether the issue specified in the complaint or the Commission's inquiry has actually been
raised in the licensee's programming.  Secondly, we
must review the licensee's determination of whether that
issue is 'controversial' and of 'public importance.'  If
these questions are answered in the affirmative, either
by admission of the licensee or by our determination
upon review, we must then determine whether the licensee has afforded a 'reasonable opportunity' in his overall programming for the presentation of contrasting
points of view."

An extract from Mr. Ginsburg's letter shows how
the Commission interpreted the law and applied it to our
particular complaint: "The Commission has never held
that the fairness doctrine is applicable to issues involving
the interpretation of religious doctrine.  While such issues may be widely and vigorously disputed in the religious community, they generally do not rise to the level of
a controversial issue of public importance.  However,

some issues while based on religious doctrine also meet
the criteria outlined above and must be considered controversial and of importance to the community at large.
You have not demonstrated that the issue involved here
meets that criteria.  Although the issue has received
media coverage in that the film itself was broadcast,
you have not shown that government and community
leaders have taken positions on the issue.  Nor have
you demonstrated that the issue has any particular impact on the community at large."


WEAKNESS OF THE LAW

A basic weakness of the fairness doctrine is that it
covers too little.  The law covers only "controversial
issues of public importance," and these are too narrowly
defined.  Why should an issue have to be controversial,
defined as "the subject of vigorous debate with substantial elements of the community in opposition to one another"?  Shouldn't all issues be presented fairly, regardless of whether they stir up a vigorous debate?
Shouldn't contrasting views of issues be presented, regardless of whether they draw much attention from government officials and other community leaders?  The
requirement that the subject be a controversial issue of
public importance makes the application of the law too
dependent on the public's moods, the fads of the moment,
and the happenstance of whether the subject attracts a
lot of attention.  A subject can be very important to society, even if the public seems unconcerned about it;
this often happens in religious and ethical matters, for
example.
The fairness doctrine does not require that each program present the opposing views, but only that the licensee's overall programming affords reasonable opportunity
for the presentation of the other views.  There are several weaknesses in this rule.  Even if the other views have

been presented, the broadcast may have been too far in the past to be effective in the current situation; some viewers may have missed the broadcast, and its coverage may have been inadequate. Or the broadcaster may claim that the other views have been presented, but not substantiate the claim.

The law places on the complainant too much responsibility for establishing the case. How much does one have to do to prove that an issue is controversial and of public importance? Take a poll? Collect newspaper clippings? Write letters? The law is vague. Many citizens do not have the time to collect such evidence and to compile a legal brief. Unlike the networks, the citizen does not have a legal staff at his command, and may lack the funds to employ an attorney. In our case, we could have and apparently should have taken polls to support our position: a poll of the public, a poll of clergymen, a poll of Old Testament professors, and a poll of historians. But if one has to go to all that trouble, why bother with FCC? Why not bring legal suit in the first place?

According to Mr. Ginsburg's letter, FCC regards issues based on religious doctrine as outside the scope of the fairness doctrine, unless they meet the criteria of the degree of media coverage, the degree of attention received from government officials and other community leaders, and the probable impact of the issue on the community at large. He also states that though "such issues may be widely and vigorously disputed in the religious community, they generally do not rise to the level of a controversial issue of public importance." Why are issues of religious doctrine any less public than other issues? Perhaps this attitude is part of the problem.


SUGGESTIONS

1. The fairness doctrine should be revised and supplemented with another law, in order to cover   clearly

the cases not now covered and those interpreted as not
covered by the present law. The terms "controversial"
and "public" should be eliminated from the fairness doc-
trine--they are too restrictive and too debatable.   In
fairness to FCC, these terms probably were included
originally to reduce the number of cases to be dealt with,
but a better way to reduce the cases is to require licen-
sees to be fair in the first place by presenting the opposing views at or near the same time as the program.   "Important" issues would be a sensible definition, but attorneys would use it as a loophole by arguing that the issue
was not important (the way they now use the terms "controversial" and "public").   The best method would be to
require that "all issues should be presented fairly, with
contrasting views at least represented on the same program, if possible; if contrasting views cannot be represented on the same program, they should be adequately
presented within three months, before or after the program."

2.   Scholars should have more input into the law.

3.   The principle should be recognized that because
television has far wider influence than other media, the
standards in television must be higher than in other media.

4.   Pseudo documentaries should be banned on television.   In other media, they should be actively discour-
aged and abundantly exposed.

5.   Broadcasters should have a firm policy of presenting all the essential facts pertaining to a subject,
presenting them accurately, and distinguishing between
fact and fiction.

6.   Broadcasters should not rely on advisories to
guide the viewers.   Advisories protect the stations and
the networks, but they do not protect the viewers.   A
better method is to correct the program itself.

There is more to the current Noah's ark nonsense than meets the eye. On the surface, it appears to be only a zealous quest for an ark on a mountain. But beneath the surface, it epitomizes a problem in religion and a problem in the media.

## NOTES

1. The Interpreter's Dictionary of the Bible (hereafter cited as IDB), vol. 2, p. 283.

2. Byron C. Nelson, The Deluge Story in Stone.

3. Byron C. Nelson, "After Its Kind," the First and Last Word on Evolution (Minneapolis, 1927).

4. André Parrot, Déluge et arche de Noé, 2d ed. (Neuchatel, 1953); ET: The Flood and Noah's Ark.

5. John Warwick Montgomery, The Quest for Noah's Ark.

6. Dave Balsiger and Charles E. Sellier, Jr., In Search of Noah's Ark.

7. Cf. ibid., chap. 1, and Montgomery, p. 295.

8. Millar Burrows, What Mean These Stones?, p. 26.

8a. Gordon Gaskill, "Mystery of Noah's Ark," p. 153.

9. W. G. Lambert and A. R. Millard, ATRA-HASĪS, p. 14.

10. Cited from ibid., pp. 143, 145; translated by M. Civil.

11. Edmond Sollberger, The Babylonian Legend of the Flood, pp. 20-21.

12. Ibid., p. 16.

13. Umberto Cassuto, A Commentary on the Book of Genesis, vol. 2, p. 5.

14. W. G. Lambert, "A New Look at the Babylonian Background of Genesis," p. 292. The earliest surviving copies are from the 17th century B.C. (Lambert and Millard, p. 23), but its original composition may be earlier.

15. Lambert and Millard, pp. 7-8.

16. Ibid., pp. 11, 15.

17. Cited from Jack Finegan, Light from the Ancient Past, 2d ed., p. 216.

18. Ibid., p. 217.

19. See Lambert and Millard, pp. 24, 131-33.

20. Nahum M. Sarna, Understanding Genesis, p. 41.

21. Lambert, "New Look," pp. 299-300.

22. E. A. Speiser, Genesis, p. 55.

23. Ibid., p. 91.

24. Cassuto, vol. 2, p. 4.

25. James G. Frazer, Folk-Lore in the Old Testament, vol. 1, pp. 148-49.

26. Ibid., p. 152.

27. Robert A. Oden, Studies in Lucian's De Syria Dea, p. 27.

28. As stated in these passages in Genesis, the period of time is from the 600th year of Noah's life, 2d month, 17th day, to the 601st year, 2d month, 27th day. The "year" is a lunar year (12 months of 29 1/2 days each), with 11 days added (according to the ancient custom of counting both the first and last days [17th and 27th]). This adds up to 365 days, a solar year. See Cassuto, vol. 2, p. 113.

29. Speiser, pp. 47-50.

30. IDB, Sup., p. 769.

31. Tertullian, On the Pallium 2.

32. Nelson, Deluge Story, p. 137.

33. Ibid., p. 152.

33a. For succinct comments on Wooley's vivid imagination and his eagerness to find whatever appealed to the Bible-reading public, see Max Mallowan, Mallowan's Memoirs, pp. 46-47, 55-56.

34. Balsiger and Sellier, pp. 45-47.

35. Ibid., pp. 44-45.

36. Cassuto, vol. 2, p. 4.

37. Enc. Britannica (Chicago, 1950), vol. 9, p. 446.

38. Ibid.

39. Madeleine S. and J. Lane Miller, Harper's Bible Dictionary (New York, 1958), p. 198.

40. John Bright, "Has Archaeology Found Evidence of the Flood?," The Biblical Archaeologist 5 (1942):60.

41. Quoted by Origen, Homily on Genesis 2. 2.

42. Quoted by Origen, Against Celsus IV. 41. Abbé Mallet in the 18th century (1751) wrestled with the logistical problems (see W. E. Rex in our "Selected Bibliog-

raphy").

43. Hermann Gunkel, The Legends of Genesis, p. 7.
44. Robert Jamieson, A Commentary: Critical, Practical, and Explanatory, on the Old and New Testaments (Chicago, 1880), vol. 1, p. 99.
45. Marcus Dods, The Book of Genesis (The Expositor's Bible, vol. 1; New York, 1905), p. 56.
46. John C. Whitcomb, Jr., and Henry M. Morris, The Genesis Flood: The Biblical Record and Its Scientific Implications, pp. 70-75.
47. Gunkel, p. 10.
48. Alexander Heidel, The Gilgamesh Epic and Old Testament Parallels, p. 250.
49. James Bryce, Transcaucasia and Ararat, p. 202. See pp. 201-204 for his discussion of the mountain traditions.
50. Josephus, Antiquities of the Jews I. 3. 5-6 (i. 89-95 in Loeb Classics).
51. Ibid.
52. Cassuto, vol. 2, p. 105.
53. According to Elmacin in the 13th century, the Christian Heraclius, Byzantine emperor early in the 7th century, climbed Mount Judi to see the place where the ark landed (Montgomery, 301). Claudius James Rich (Narrative of a Residence in Koordistan, . . ., vol. 2, pp. 123-26) described the region around Mount Judi early in the 19th century.
54. Cassuto, pp. 29, 105; Heidel, p. 235.
55. Julius Africanus, Chronography 4.
56. Theophilus, To Autolycus III. 19.
57. Julius Africanus, Chronography 4.
58. Heidel, p. 251.
59. Bryce, p. 212.
60. Ibid., p. 250.
61. Montgomery, p. 266.
62. Bryce, p. 206.
63. Ibid., p. 293.
64. Josephus, Antiquities I. 3. 6 (i. 93 in Loeb).

65. Ibid., XX. 2. 2 (xx. 24-25 in Loeb Classics).

66. Theophilus, To Autolycus III. 19.

67. Hippolytus, Refutation of All Heresies X. 26.

68. Chrysostom, On Perfect Charity (in Migne PG, vol. 56, cols. 287-88).

69. Epiphanius, Panarion I. 1. 18.

70. In Ante-Nicene Fathers, vol. 5, p. 198.

71. My summary of the legend is based upon Montgomery's translation (pp. 66-69) of Jean-Baptiste Emine's French translation.

72. Balsiger and Sellier, p. 80.

72a. Montgomery, pp. 75-78.

73. Sir John Mandeville, The Travels of Sir John Mandeville, chap. 16, p. 100.

74. Adam Olearius, Travels, book IV, p. 139 in 1669 ed.

75. Jan J. Struys, Voiages and Travels, chap. 18, pp. 212-18.

76. See Montgomery, "Appendix A."

77. Ibid., p. 81.

78. C. J. Rich, Narrative of a Residence in Koordistan, vol. 2, p. 124.

79. Bryce, pp. 265-66.

80. Montgomery, p. 105.

81. Gordon Gaskill, "The Mystery of Noah's Ark," p. 153.

82. A. Parrot, p. 65.

83. Bright, p. 59.

84. A. Parrot, p. 64, n. 4.

85. Montgomery, p. 292 and "Appendix C."

86. Ibid., pp. 114-18.

87. Balsiger and Sellier, pp. 102-105.

88. Carveth Wells, Kapoot, pp. 223-29.

89. Balsiger and Sellier, pp. 157-59.

90. Werner Keller, The Bible as History, pp. 58-59; Balsiger and Sellier, pp. 155.

91. Balsiger and Sellier, pp. 155-56.

92. Ibid., pp. 159-60.

93.  Cited from A. Parrot, p. 65.

93a.  Keller, p. 59.

94.  Cited from A. Parrot, p. 65.

95.  Montgomery, pp. 121-24.

96.  Navarra's report quoted by Balsiger and Sellier, pp. 169-70.

97.  Montgomery presents only a drawing of it, made by his young son, and states that it cannot be reproduced in his book "for security reasons." Balsiger and Sellier, however, reproduce the photograph and an enlargement of the portion showing the object (27th page of the 32-page section of photos).

98.  Balsiger and Sellier, pp. 200-201; Montgomery, p. 263.

99.  Balsiger and Sellier, the 28th page in the photograph section; see also p. 164.

100.  Gaskill, p. 152.

101.  From Bryce, pp. 208-209, 239-40.

102.  From Wells, pp. 196-98.

103.  Ibid., pp. 224-28.

104.  Ibid., p. 224; Friedrich Parrot, Journey to Ararat, pp. 101-102.

105.  Floyd R. Bailey, "Wood from 'Mount Ararat': Noah's Ark?," p. 138.

106.  Bailey, pp. 138-41 (a corresponding chapter reportedly will be in his book  Where Is Noah's Ark?). See this article or chapter for an excellent description of the tests and their validity.

107.  Bailey, p. 142.

108.  Ibid., pp. 143-45.  For an example of the unwarranted attack on the carbon 14 test, see Balsiger and Sellier, pp. 186-90.

109.  See Time, June 27, 1977, p. 72.

110.  The story is reported in Balsiger and Sellier, pp. 89-91, and in Gaskill, p. 153.

111.  Cited from Gaskill, p. 154.

112.  New Yorker, Nov. 27, 1971, p. 181.

113.  A recent Washington Post Special reports that

the U.S. Department of Agriculture has just spent $28,000
to produce a 14-minute film to counteract the scare potential of "Swarm," lest people think that all bees are potential killers and should be destroyed (Chicago Sun-Times,
July 19, 1978, p. 24).

114. Ronald Story, The Space-gods Revealed: A
Close Look at the Theories of Erich von Däniken. New
York: Harper and Row, 1976. Von Däniken promotes
his views through the Ancient Astronaut Society; it held
its Fifth World Conference in Chicago July 27-29, 1978,
at which he was the featured speaker.

115. The quotations are from Frank Swertlow's
column in tv news (in Chicago Daily News) for the week
of Dec. 31, 1977-Jan. 7, 1978, pp 4-5.

116. The authors of the book had prominent roles
in the writing and production of the film.

117. Speiser, pp. 75-76.

118. See in our "Selected Bibliography" the entries
under Hickey, "Steve Allen," and "TV's Courtship."

119. TV Guide, April 22, 1978, pp. 8, 10.

120. Ibid., p. 10.

121. "Steve Allen. . .," p. 76.

122. See Karl E. Meyer, "Arledge Leads the Way,"
Saturday Review, August 1978, p. 39.

123. Listed in our "Selected Bibliography" under
U.S. Federal Communications Commission.

124. See "The FCC: Washington's Worst Agency?"
in the "Selected Bibliography" below.

# SELECTED BIBLIOGRAPHY

## TEXTS OF THE FLOOD STORY

Apollodorus. The Library. ET by Sir James George
Frazer. Vol. 1. (Loeb Classical Library) Cam-
bridge, MA: Harvard University Press, 1967.

Atrahasis. ATRA-HASĪS: The Babylonian Story of the
Flood, by W. G. Lambert and A. R. Millard, with
the Sumerian Flood Story, by M. Civil. Oxford:
Clarendon Press, 1969.

The Bible.

Heidel, Alexander. The Gilgamesh Epic and Old Testament Parallels. 2d ed. Chicago: University of
Chicago Press, 1963.

Kramer, Samuel Noah. History Begins at Sumer.
Garden City, NY: Doubleday, 1959.

Lucianus Samosatensis [Lucian of Samosata]. The
Syrian Goddess (De Dea Syria) Attributed to Lucian.
ET by Harold W. Attridge and Robert A. Oden.
Missoula: Scholars Press, 1976.

Mendelsohn, Isaac, ed. Religions of the Ancient Near
East: Sumero-Akkadian Religious Texts and Ugaritic Epics. New York: Liberal Arts Press, 1955.

Ovid. Metamorphoses. ET by Frank Justus Miller.
2d ed. Vol. 1. (Loeb Classical Library) Cam-
bridge, MA: Harvard University Press, 1921.

Pritchard, James B., ed. Ancient Near Eastern Texts
Relating to the Old Testament. 3d ed. Princeton:
Princeton University Press, 1969.

## ORTHODOX APPROACH

Balsiger, Dave, and Charles E. Sellier, Jr. In Search
of Noah's Ark. Los Angeles: Sun Classic Books,
1976.

Cohen, H. Hirsch. The Drunkenness of Noah. University, AL: University of Alabama Press, 1974.

Filby, Frederick A.  The Flood Reconsidered: A review of the evidences of geology, archaeology, ancient literature and the Bible.  (Contemporary Evangelical Persectives)  Grand Rapids: Zondervan Publishing House, 1971.

"In Search of Noah's Ark."  Film produced by Sun Classic Pictures, Inc.  Charles E. Sellier, Jr., producer. Los Angeles, 1976.

Keller, Werner.  The Bible as History: Archaeology Confirms the Book of Books.  Tr. from the German by Wm. Neil.  London: Hodder & Stoughton, 1956.

La Haye, T., and J. Morris.  The Ark on Ararat. Nashville: Thomas Nelson, 1976.

Marston, Charles, Sir.  The Bible Is True: The Lessons of the 1925-1934 Excavations in Bible Lands Summarized and Explained.  London: Eyre and Spottiswoode, 1934.

Montgomery, John Warwick.  The Quest for Noah's Ark. Minneapolis: Bethany Fellowship, 1972.

Navarra, Fernand.  J'ai trouvé l'arche de Noé.  [I Have Found the Ark of Noah]  Paris: Éditions France-Empire, 1956.

----------------.  Noah's Ark, I Touched It.  Edited by Dave Balsiger.  Tr. by Richard Utt.  Plainfield, NJ: Logos International, 1974.

Nelson, Byron C.  The Deluge Story in Stone: A History of the Flood Theory of Geology.  Minneapolis: Augsburg Publishing House, 1931.

Unger, Merrill F.  Archaeology and the Old Testament. Grand Rapids: Zondervan, 1954.

Whitcomb, John C., Jr., and Henry M. Morris.  The Genesis Flood: The Biblical Record and Its Scientific Implications.  Philadelphia: Presbyterian and Reformed Publishing Co., 1961.

## HISTORICAL APPROACH

Adelsen, Charles. "Land of Great Ararat: Turkey's Forbidden Territory." Geographical Magazine 42 (1969):188-93.

Allen, Don Cameron. The Legend of Noah: Renaissance Rationalism in Art, Science and Letters. Urbana: University of Illinois Press, 1949.

"Ararat 'ark' wood dated at A. D. 700." Science News 111 (Mar. 26, 1977):198-99.

Bailey, Lloyd R. "Wood from 'Mt. Ararat': Noah's Ark?" Biblical Archaeologist 40 (1977):137-46.

Barr, James. Fundamentalism. Philadelphia: Westminster Press, 1978.

Bright, John. "Has Archaeology Found Evidence of the Flood?" The Biblical Archaeologist 5 (1942):55-62.

Bryce, James. Transcaucasia and Ararat: Being Notes of a Vacation Tour in the Autumn of 1876. London: Macmillan, 1877.

Budge, E. A. Wallis. The Babylonian Story of the Deluge and the Epic of Gilgamesh. London: British Museum, 1920.

Burrows, Millar. What Mean These Stones? The Significance of Archaeology for Biblical Studies. New York: Meridian Books, 1957.

Cassuto, Umberto. A Commentary on the Book of Genesis. Part II, From Noah to Abraham. Tr. by Israel Abrahams. Jerusalem: Magnes Press, 1964.

Clemens, Samuel Langhorne. Letters from the Earth. New York: Harper & Row, 1962. [not historical study, but humorous questioning of the Flood, in Letters 4-7]

"Expedition Seeks to Recover Remains of Noah's Ark." The Christian Century 87 (1970):72.

Finegan, Jack. Light from the Ancient Past: The Archeological Background of the Hebrew-Christian Religion. 2d ed. Princeton: Princeton University Press, 1959.

Frazer, James, Sir. Folk-Lore in the Old Testament.
    Vol. 1. London: Macmillan, 1918.
Gaskill, Gordon. "The Mystery of Noah's Ark." Read-
    er's Digest 107, no. 9 (Sept. 1975):150-54. Con-
    densed from Christian Herald, Aug. 1975.
Gillispie, Charles Coulston. Genesis and Geology: A
    Study in the Relations of Scientific Thought, Natural
    Theology, and Social Opinion in Great Britain, 1790-
    1850. Cambridge, MA: Harvard University Press,
    1951.
Gunkel, Hermann. The Legends of Genesis. Tr. by W.
    H. Carruth. Chicago: Open Court, 1907.
Halliday, William R., Sir. "Folklore." Encyclopaedia
    Britannica. Vol. 9. Chicago: Encyclopaedia Bri-
    tannica, 1950.
"In the wake of the ark." Science News 97 (1970):574.
    [issue date: June 13, 1970]
The Interpreter's Dictionary of the Bible. 4 vols. Nash-
    ville and New York: Abingdon, 1962. Sup., 1976.
Jacobsen, Thorkild. The Sumerian King List. Chicago:
    University of Chicago Press, 1939.
----------------. The Treasures of Darkness: A
    History of Mesopotamian Religion. New Haven and
    London: Yale University Press, 1976.
Jamieson, Robert. A Commentary: Critical, Practical,
    and Explanatory, on the Old and New Testaments.
    Vol. 1. Chicago: Fairbanks, 1880.
Jastrow, Morris, Jr. Hebrew and Babylonian Traditions.
    New York: Scribners, 1914.
Jeremias, Alfred. The Old Testament in the Light of
    the Ancient East. Tr. by C. L. Beaumont. Vol. 1.
    London: Williams and Norgate, 1911.
Kenyon, Frederic George, Sir. The Bible and Archae-
    ology. New York and London: Harper, 1940.
King, Leonard William. Legends of Babylon and Egypt
    in Relation to Hebrew Tradition. London: Oxford
    University Press, 1918.
Kraeling, Emil G. "Xisouthros, Deucalion and the Flood

Traditions." Journal of the American Oriental Society 67 (1947): 177-83.

Laessøe, Jørgen. "The Atrahasis Epic, a Babylonian History of Mankind." Biblioteca Orientalis 13 (1956):90-102.

Lambert, W. G. "A New Look at the Babylonian Background of Genesis." Journal of Theological Studies, N.S. 16 (1965):287-300.

Lewis, Jack P. A Study of the Interpretation of Noah and the Flood in Jewish and Christian Literature. Leiden: Brill, 1968.

Mallowan, Max. Mallowan's Memoirs. New York: Dodd, Mead, 1977.

------------. "Noah's Flood Reconsidered." Iraq 26 (1964):62-82.

Mandeville, John, Sir. The Travels of Sir John Mandeville. The version of the Cotton Manuscript in modern spelling. London: Macmillan, 1905.

Marty, Martin E. "Noah and the Arkeologists." The Christian Century 93:1063. [issue date: Nov. 24, 1976]

"Noah's Ark?" Life 49 (Sept. 5, 1960):112, 114.

Oden, Robert A., Jr. Studies in Lucian's De Syria Dea. (Harvard Semitic Monographs, 15) Missoula: Scholars Press, 1977.

Olearius, Adam. The Voyages and Travels of the Ambassadors Sent by Frederick Duke of Holstein, to the Great Duke of Muscovy, and the King of Persia. Tr. by John Davies. 2d ed., cor. London: Starkey and Basset, 1669.

Parrot, André. The Flood and Noah's Ark. Tr.from 2d French ed. by Edwin Hudson. London: SCM Press, 1955.

Parrot, Friedrich. Journey to Ararat. Tr. by W. D. Cooley. London: Longman, Brown, Green, and Longmans, 1845.

Rad, Gerhard von. Genesis: A Commentary. Tr. by J. H. Marks. London: SCM Press, 1961.

Rex, Walter E. "'Arche de Noé' and Other Religious
    Articles by Abbé Mallet in the Encyclopédie." Eigh-
    teenth Century Studies 9 (1975/76): 333-52.
Rich, Claudius James. Narrative of a Residence in
    Koordistan, and on the Site of Ancient Nineveh; with
    Journal of a Voyage down the Tigris to Bagdad and
    an Account of a Visit to Shirauz and Persepolis.
    Ed. by his Widow. Vol. 2. London: James Duncan,
    1836.
Sarna, Nahum M. Understanding Genesis. (The Heritage
    of Biblical Israel, 1) New York: Jewish Theological
    Seminary of America and McGraw-Hill, 1966.
Smith, John Pye. On the Relation Between the Holy
    Scriptures and Some Parts of Geological Science.
    London: Jackson and Walford, 1839.
Sollberger, Edmond. The Babylonian Legend of the
    Flood. 3d ed. London: British Museum, 1971.
Speiser, Ephraim A. Genesis. Garden City, NY:
    Doubleday, 1964.
Struys, Jan Janszoon. The Voiages and Travels through
    Italy, Greece, Muscovy, Tartary, Media, Persia,
    East-India, Japan, and Other Countries in Europe,
    Africa and Asia. Tr. by John Mossison. London:
    A. Swalle, 1684.
Thompson, Thomas L. The Historicity of the Patri-
    archal Narratives: The Quest for the Historical
    Abraham. Berlin: de Gruyter, 1974.
Van Seters, John. Abraham in History and Tradition.
    New Haven and London: Yale University Press,
    1975.
Wells, Carveth. Kapoot: The Narrative of a Journey
    from Leningrad to Mount Ararat in Search of Noah's
    Ark. London: Jarrold Publishers, 1934.
Woolley, Leonard, Sir. Excavations at Ur. London:
    Ernest Benn Ltd., 1954.

TELEVISION

"The FCC: Washington's Worst Agency?" U.S. News and World Report, 30 January 1978, pp. 37-40.

Hickey, Neil. "Changing the Shape of Television." TV Guide, 22 and 29 April, 6 May 1978.

Meyer, Karl E. "Arledge Leads the Way." Saturday Review, Aug. 1978, p. 39.

"Steve Allen: TV Is 'Junk Food for the Mind.'" U.S. News and World Report, 13 March 1978, pp. 76-77.

"TV's Courtship of Turned-off Viewers." U.S. News and World Report, 30 Jan. 1978, p. 54.

U.S. Federal Communications Commission. "Fairness Doctrine and Public Interest Standards: Fairness Report Regarding Handling of Public Issues." Federal Register, vol. 39, no. 139 (18 July 1978): 26,372-90.

U.S. Federal Communications Commission. Federal Communications Commission Policy Concerning the Fairness Doctrine and Procedures to Be Used in Filing Fairness Doctrine Complaints. (Informational Memorandum) Washington, D.C.: n. d.